AbleMUSE
A REVIEW OF POETRY, PROSE & ART

NUMBER 17
Summer 2014

TRANSLATION
Anthology Issue

Guest Editor
Charles Martin

www.ablemuse.com

Able Muse Press
publishing the new, the established

Now available from Able Muse Press:

Able Muse Anthology
Edited by Alexander Pepple
Foreword by Timothy Steele

978-0-9865338-0-8 • $16.95

With R.S. Gwynn, Rhina P. Espaillat, Rachel Hadas, Mark Jarman, Timothy Murphy, Dick Davis, A.E. Stallings, Alan Sullivan, Deborah Warren, Diane Thiel, Leslie Monsour, Kevin Durkin, Turner Cassity, Kim Bridgford, Richard Moore and others.

". . . Here's a generous serving of the cream of Able Muse including not only formal verse but nonmetrical work that also displays careful craft, memorable fiction (seven remarkable stories), striking artwork and photography, and incisive prose." — X.J. Kennedy

Able Muse - Inaugural Print Edition

WITH:

POEMS, FICTION, BOOK REVIEWS, INTERVIEWS & ESSAYS from catherine tufariello ▪ catharine savage brosman ▪ leslie monsour ▪ ned balbo ▪ ted mc carthy ▪ diane seuss ▪ susan mclean ▪ rebecca foust ▪ j. patrick lewis ▪ john slater ▪ gail white ▪ kim bridgford ▪ nancy lou canyon ▪ john whitworth ▪ peter filkins ▪ marilyn l. taylor ▪ and others

ISBN 978-0-9865338-2-2

Subscribe to: *Able Muse (Print Ed.)*

~ **Print Edition** ~

Semiannual review of poetry, prose & art

Able Muse (Print Edition) continues the excellence in poetry, art, fiction, essays, interviews and book reviews we've brought you all these years in the online edition. Subscribe at *www.ablemusepress.com*

For complete details, visit: **www.AbleMusePress.com**

visit Able Muse

online for more than a decade of archives, plus web-only features not available in the print edition at:

www.ablemuse.com

Able Muse is not just another poetry site. It is one of the best sites on the Internet.
—Heather O'Neil, *Suite101.com*

Eratosphere
A forum of Able Muse Review

Able Muse's premier online forums and workshops for metrical and non-metrical poetry, fiction, translations, art, nonfiction and discussions at:

http://eratosphere.ablemuse.com

Able Muse and its extraordinary companion website, the *Eratosphere,* have created a huge and influential virtual literary community. —Dana Gioia

Able Muse
www.ablemuse.com

Guest Editor	Charles Martin
Guest Associate Editor	Janice D. Soderling
Editor	Alexander Pepple
Assistant Poetry Editors	Peter Austin, Reagan Upshaw
Nonfiction Editor	Gregory Dowling
Fiction Editor	Karen Kevorkian
Assistant Fiction Editors	John Riley, Janice D. Soderling, Rob Wright
Editorial Board	Rachel Hadas, X.J. Kennedy, A.E. Stallings, Timothy Steele, Deborah Warren

Able Muse is published semiannually. Subscription rates for individuals: $24.00 per year; libraries and institutions: $34 per year; single and previous issues: $16.95 + $3 S&H. International subscription rate: $33 per year; single and previous issues: $16.95 + $5 S&H. Subscribe online at www.ablemusepress.com or send a check payable to *Able Muse Review* to the snail mail address indicated below. (USD throughout. Online payment with PayPal/credit card.)

We read year-round and welcome previously unpublished manuscripts only. No simultaneous submissions. Online or email submissions ONLY. Submission guidelines available at: www.ablemuse.com/submit

Queries and other correspondence should be emailed to: editor@ablemuse.com
For paper correspondence, be sure to include a self-addressed, stamped envelope.

Library of Congress Control Number: 2014939711

ISBN 978-1-927409-45-9 (paperback) / ISBN 978-1-927409-46-6 (digital)

ISSN 2168-0426

Cover image: "Element Fire" by Cathrine Langwagen

Cover & book design by Alexander Pepple

Attn: Alexander Pepple, Editor
Able Muse Review
467 Saratoga Avenue #602
San Jose, CA 95129

www.ablemuse.com
editor@ablemuse.com

Printed in the United States of America
Published in 2014 by Able Muse Press: www.ablemusepress.com

Alexander Pepple

Editorial

This first special issue of *Able Muse* focuses on the theme of translation. We are honored to bring you a translation anthology in which some of the most skilled translators practicing today are represented. The issue is guest edited, with our thanks, by acclaimed poet and translator, Charles Martin. We are also grateful for the diligence, expertise, and eclectic talents of one of our assistant fiction editors, Janice D. Soderling, who took on the additional task of associate editor for this issue.

Almost all of our past issues have included one or more translations. In fact the translation forum of *Eratosphere*, *Able Muse*'s online workshop, has remained a popular venue over the years for practicing the craft of translation, although it has been somewhat of a niche activity there compared to *Eratosphere*'s regular goings-on. Still, this changes at least yearly with our Translation Bake-off, and with flurries of activity such as that centering on the question of what to do for rhyme (or not) in Rilke's "Archaic Torso of Apollo," if you're going to render the concluding *"Du mußt dein Leben ändern"* as "You must change your life." Such conundrums are not always a concern for the translations in this issue, as selected by our guest editor Charles Martin—his picks include prose poems in addition to free and formal verse. The same is true of the translation methods represented, which range from faithfully mirroring stanza patterns down to the meter and rhyme; to compression of page-long verse into a couple of quatrains; to the explosion of a sonnet into twice as many lines or more; to adaptations; to imitations; to culling of passages and lines from one or more poems of the original into a hybridized adaptation. Although the majority of the translations are from individual contributors, we also have some that are the products of the collaboration between two or more translators, and even one such collaboration that involves the original author.

While multiculturalism has become something of a rallying cry today, and often overextended to the point of cliché, world poetry is invariably multicultural. In this translation anthology, our guest editor has braved an influx of submitted material, boldly wading through a daunting slush pile, and expertly choosing the best poems from an appealingly diverse mix—from various corners of the world, from various points in history, from what is unusual, startling, inspirational, or time-honored. Through the medium of modern English, all are made accessible to a typical reader of *Able Muse*. We thank everyone who responded to our call for translations and submitted. The multifarious depth and richness of the material available to choose from is what has made this a special translation issue indeed.

As for who is translated here, they span the gamut from poets of early antiquity to some still living, and across several languages old and new, from Arabic to Old English to Yiddish. Regardless of the approach or methodology that produced them, these translations are English poems in their own right. In the interest of having space to present more poems, we did not include the text for the original poems.

We will be going back to our regular issue and release schedule starting with the next issue, Winter 2014. Now, we hope that you enjoy this special issue as much as we've enjoyed bringing it to you. Next, a few words about our guest editor Charles Martin, followed by his introduction to this translation anthology.

The very best,

Alexander Pepple
—Editor

BOOKS
FROM
ABLE MUSE PRESS

NEW & RECENT RELEASES

MELISSA BALMAIN
Walking in on People - Poems
~ WINNER, 2013 ABLE MUSE BOOK AWARD ~

ELLEN KAUFMAN
House Music - Poems

BARBARA ELLEN SORENSEN
Compositions of the Dead Playing Flutes - Poems

FRANK OSEN
Virtue, Big as Sin - Poems
~ WINNER, 2012 ABLE MUSE BOOK AWARD ~

JAMES POLLOCK
Sailing to Babylon - Poems

MATTHEW BUCKLEY SMITH
Dirge for an Imaginary World - Poems
~ WINNER, 2011 ABLE MUSE BOOK AWARD ~

APRIL LINDNER
This Bed Our Bodies Shaped - Poems

JAMES RICHARD WAKEFIELD
A Vertical Mile - Poems

MICHAEL CANTOR
Life in the Second Circle - Poems

HOLLIS SEAMON
Corporeality - Stories

CAROL LIGHT
Heaven from Steam - Poems

STEPHEN SCAER
Pumpkin Chucking - Poems

MARYANN CORBETT
Credo for the Checkout Line in Winter - Poems

WENDY VIDELOCK
The Dark Gnu and Other Poems

BEN BERMAN
Strange Borderlands - Poems

CATHERINE CHANDLER
Lines of Flight - Poems

MARGARET ANN GRIFFITHS
Grasshopper: The Poetry of M A Griffiths

WENDY VIDELOCK
Nevertheless - Poems

AARON POOCHIGIAN
The Cosmic Purr - Poems

LATEST ABLE MUSE PRESS CATALOG
Free Download at: www.ablemusepress.com/catalog

CHARLES MARTIN's most recent book of poems is *Signs & Wonders*, published in 2011 by Johns Hopkins University Press. His verse translation of the *Metamorphoses of Ovid* (2004) received the Harold Morton Landon Award from the Academy of American Poets. In 2005, he received an Award for Literature from the American Academy of Arts and Letters. He served as Poet in Residence at The Cathedral of St. John the Divine in New York from 2005 to 2009.

Charles Martin

Guest Editorial

W. H. Auden wrote that whenever he wished to discourage conversation with someone seated next to him on a plane, he would answer, "Medieval historian," when that person asked what it was that he did. The response would inevitably send his neighbor back to his reading. Those of us engaged in the practice of poetic translation need not stoop to such mendacities in order to discourage unwanted intimacies. From experience, I can guarantee that, on almost any imaginable social occasion, all that it takes to shake someone off is to respond to the 'What do you do' question, with something like, "At the moment I'm working with a Sanskrit scholar on a translation of a Hindu religious poem called. . . ." The sentence rarely gets completed, as one's interlocutor suddenly discovers an empty glass in hand or a long-lost friend on the other side of the room and quickly leaves one to the bliss of solitude.

Perhaps naively, I find this reaction puzzling, since translating poetry is no more arcane an activity than reading or writing it: it combines an intense kind of reading with a kind of writing that is perhaps a little bit less intense than writing one's own poetry: the content, after all, is always there, waiting. Besides, for those of us who translate poetry from one language to another, the activity itself is an endless source of fascinating discourse, and has been ever since John Dryden raised the subject in the 17th century. Dryden, famously, divided the translation of poetry into three parts, which he called metaphrase (word for word translation), paraphrase (not word-for word, but following the sense of the original) and imitation—an approach he thought so free as to perhaps wriggle out of the bonds of translation altogether.

Almost everyone who has followed in Dryden's footsteps has followed the same tripartite division, though with the borders between metaphrase and imitation sliding back and forth in the 20th century like the borders of Poland or Lithuania. What Dryden or Pope considered strict paraphrase, we might very well think of as free imitation. Nevertheless, the division has held, and anyone interested in seeing the latest theoretical developments in that division should read *The Poetics of Translation* by Willis Barnstone, one of the distinguished contributors to this issue.

Given the choice between metaphrase, paraphrase and imitation, there has been a tendency across the ages for most poet-translators to seek out the middle ground and congregate in paraphrase. Metaphrase, word-for-word translation, sounds as though it should be the ideal. Perhaps its most famous literary example is Nabokov's version of *Eugene Onegin*. But whatever virtues his translation may have, it does no honor to Pushkin's style, and finding a style that will respond in some way to one's author's is no small part of what a literary translator does. Imitation, the oldest form of literary translation, and the process that is closest to the process by which we write our own poetry, is harder to dismiss. Certainly, we would all be the poorer without such great modern examples of it as Robert Lowell's *Imitations*, or Ezra Pound's *Cathay*, or Christopher Logue's versions of the *Iliad*. And many of us had our first exposure to Shakespeare's *The Tempest* in the cinematic form of *Forbidden Planet*. How bad was that? At its best (as in the example of Robert Lowell's work) it seems to be a kind of dialogue between source and translator that the reader is privileged to eavesdrop on; at its most outrageous, it can be a form of cultural exploitation.

It certainly seems to be so for those poet-translators who, as Vikram Seth puts it, "admit the primacy of the original and attempt fidelity to it." They seek to create a style, either analogous or mimetic, that will respond to their original. Most of the work selected for this special translation issue of *Able Muse* is of this kind; Dryden would see it as paraphrase. But because we need to be shaken up from time to time and to have our assumptions challenged, some of what he might have thought of as imitations have also been included. If the proportion is weighted in favor of paraphrase, that has more to do with the gifts and inclinations of the contributors than with the selection process.

It remains for me to thank Alexander Pepple for inviting me to be guest editor of this translation issue of Able Muse, and to thank him and Janice D. Soderling for all of the work they have done to make it possible. And finally, to thank our contributors, whose superb accomplishment as poet-translators you have only to turn the pages to discover.

Charles Martin
—Guest Editor

CONTENTS

Alexander Pepple
    EDITORIAL / V

Charles Martin
    GUEST EDITORIAL / IX

ESSAYS

Michael Palma
    "AGAINST THE DAILY GRIND" / 112

POETRY TRANSLATIONS

William Baer

Translated from the Portuguese of
Fernando Pessoa
    AUTOPSYCHOGRAPHY / 1

Translated from the Spanish of
Miguel de Unamuno
    PORTUGAL / 2

Translated from the Latin of
Catullus
    CARMEN CI / 3

Ned Balbo

Adapted from the French of
Charles Baudelaire
    THE DISPOSSESSED / 4
    DON JUAN IN HELL / 5
    WINTER BELL / 7

Tony Barnstone

Translated from the Greek of
C.P. Cavafy
    WALLS / 8

Translated from the Italian of
Francesco Petrarch
    SONNET 13 / 9

Translated from the German of
Rainer Maria Rilke
    THE PANTHER / 10

Tony Barnstone and *Bilal Shaw*

Translated from the Urdu of
Asadullah Khan Ghalib
    HEAVEN'S TEETH / 11

Willis Barnstone

Translated from the Latin of
Horace
    WEATHERVANE / 12
    WINTER BREAKING UP / 14
    COLD WINTER / 16
    ENJOY THE DAY / 18
    O SHIP, THE WAVES
      ARE SWEEPING YOU / 19
    INVITATION / 21
    HIGHHANDED MATCHMAKING / 22
    CLEOPATRA / 24

Mark S. Bauer

Translated from the Latin of
Martial
    MARTIAL II:53 / 26
    PARCERE PERSONIS,
      DICERE DEVITIIS / 27

Michael Bradburn-Ruster

Translated from the Spanish of
José Luis Puerto
    THE HOUSE / 28
    CHESTNUT TREE / 30

Heidi Czerwiec and *Claudia Routon*

Translated from the Spanish of
José Corredor-Matheos
    BEFORE A PAINTING BY
      JORDI PALLARÉS / 31
    BEFORE A STILL LIFE BY
      JUAN VAN DER HAMEN / 33
    BEFORE A PAINTING BY
      MARC ROTHKO / 34

Brett Foster

Translated from the Italian of
Cecco Angiolieri
    HEDGING MY BETS / 36
    THE MARRIAGE OF ROPE
      AND ROOF BEAM / 37
    SEE YOU, WOULDN'T WANT
      TO BE YOU / 38

Catherine Chandler

Translated from the Spanish of
Delmira Agustini
    MY LOVES / 39

Terese Coe
Translated from the German of
Heinrich Heine
- Happiness / 43

Maryann Corbett
Translated from the French of
Christine de Pizan
- Ballade IV from Les Cent Ballades / 44
- Ballade VII from Les Cent Ballades / 46
- Ballade LIX from Les Cent Ballades / 48
- Ballade LXXXVI from Les Cent Ballades / 50

Dick Davis
Translated from the Persian
Five Poems by Women Writing in Persian
- Nur Jahan / 52
- Jahan Khanom / 52
- Ayesheh-ye afghan / 52
- Ayesheh-ye afghan / 53
- Reshheh / 53

Adam Elgar
Translated from the Italian of
Gaspara Stampa
- Rime 4 / 55
- Rime 5 / 56
- Rime 8 / 57
- Rime 21 / 58
- Rime 31 / 59

Andrew Frisardi
Translated from the Italian of
Dante Alighieri
- "Amor che ne la mente mi ragiona" / 60

Diane Furtney
Translated from the French of
Arthur Rimbaud
- Vowels / 66

Translated from the French of
Armand Sully Prudhomme
- The Rendezvous / 68

Translated from the French of
Gérard de Nerval
- And It Vanishes / 70

Adapted from the French of
François Villon
- What Lasts / 72

Rachel Hadas
Translated from the Greek of
Euripides
IPHIGENIA IN AULIS / 74

Jay Hopler
Translated from the German of
Georg Trakl
THE RATS / 79
EVENING THUNDERSTORM / 80
AMEN / 81

Teresa Iverson
Translated from the German of
Nelly Sachs
FIVE POEMS / 82

Julie Kane, *with the author* and Rima Krasauskytė
Translated from the Lithuanian of
Tautvyda Marcinkevičiūtė
THE HARDEST WORK / 90

Julie Kane
Translated from the French of
Victor Hugo
SHE PICKED UP THE HABIT / 92

X.J. Kennedy
Translated from the French of
Arthur Rimbaud
SENSATION / 94
EVIL / 95
MY SAD HEART SNIVELS ON THE POOP / 96

Kent Leatham
Translated from the Scots of
Gavin Douglas
FROM BOOK 7 OF *ENEADOS* / 98

Translated from the Scots of
William Fowler
SONNET: IN ORKNEY / 100

Translated from the Scots of
William Dunbar
THE TWO OLD NAGS / 101

R.C. Neighbors
Translated from the German of
Bertolt Brecht
OF THE DROWNED GIRL / 103

Kate Light and Michael Palma
Translated from the Italian of
Antonio Malatesti
RIDDLES / 105

Michael Palma
Translated from the Italian of
Giovanni Raboni
  "Sono quello che eravate..." / 107
  "Fra l'Anschluss e la notte dei cristalli..." / 108
  "La casa di campagna..." / 109

Translated from the Italian of
Fosildo Mirtunzio (Pseudonym)
  Riddles / 110

Deborah Ann Percy and Arnold Johnston, with Dona Roşu
Translated from the Romanian of
Zaharia Stancu
  The Days, The Days / 117
  The Fourth Horse / 119
  Man at Sunset / 121

Maria Picone
Translated from the French of
Rainer Maria Rilke
  Circus Performers / 125
  For Monique / 126
  Prose Poem / 128
  Melon / 129
  Cemetery / 130

John Ridland
Translated from the French of
Paul Valéry
  The Seaside Cemetery at Sète / 131

Robert Schechter
Translated from the Danish of
Tove Ditlevsen
  A Woman's Fear / 138

Translated from the Spanish of
Sor Juana Inés de la Cruz
  To Her Portrait / 140
  She'd Rather Die than Expose Herself to the Outrage of Growing Old / 141

Wendy Sloan
Translated from the Italian of
Giacomo Leopardi
  To Sylvia / 142

A.E. Stallings
Translated from the Greek of
Hesiod
  The Five Races of Man / 145

Translated from the Greek of
C.P. Cavafy
  Interruption / 149

Jeff Sypeck

Translated from the Latin of
Paul the Deacon
- EPITAPH FOR THE BABY HILDEGARD, DAUGHTER OF CHARLEMAGNE AND QUEEN HILDEGARD / *150*

N.S. Thompson

Translated from the Italian of
Giovanni Pascoli
- OCTOBER EVENING / *151*
- NOVEMBER / *152*

John Whitworth

Translated from the Greek of
Meleager
- TWO EPIGRAMS / *153*

Ryan Wilson

Translated from the Spanish of
Lope de Vega
- TOMORROW / *155*

Translated from the French of
Charles Baudelaire
- EXOTIC PERFUME / *156*

Shifra Zisman *and* Laine Zisman Newman

Translated from the Yiddish of
Dovid Zisman
- A SPARK OF FREEDOM / *158*

RIDDLE NOTES / *175*

CONTRIBUTOR NOTES / *177*

INDEX / *201*

Strange Borderlands
Poems
by Ben Berman

*NEW~ from Able Muse Press

SHORTLISTED:
2014 Massachusetts Book Award

PRAISE FOR *STRANGE BORDERLANDS*
(*with a Foreword by Fred Marchant*)

★★★★★

"Ben Berman's debut poetry collection is a compelling examination of the author's experiences in Zimbabwe as a Peace Corps volunteer. . . . This is a must-have book for readers of poetry." — *Publishers Weekly*, Starred Review

"Ben Berman's lyric poems set in Zimbabwe dig deep into the casual and the casualty of daily life . . . This is an unforgettable debut by a powerful and humble voice."
— *Dzvinia Orlowsky*

"These are poems that weigh, consider, and restore some flesh-and-blood meaning to the experience of multiculturalism, a word so overused it is often flattened out to a platitude or piety. But not in this book."
— *Fred Marchant (from the "Foreword")*

"What's most impressive about this terrific book is Berman's inclusive generous spirit, the deadly serious imaginative play he exercises in every line of every poem. This is a book to cherish."
— *Alan Shapiro*

ISBN 978-1-927409-03-9 / 104 pages

ORDER NOW FROM ABLE MUSE PRESS AT: WWW.ABLEMUSEPRESS.COM
OR, ORDER FROM AMAZON.COM, BN.COM, . . . & OTHER ONLINE OR OFFLINE BOOKSTORES

www.AbleMusePress.com

William Baer
Translated from the Portuguese of
Fernando Pessoa
1888 – 1935

Autopsychography

The poet is a faker,
whose faking is so real,
he even fakes the pain
he actually can feel.

And those who read his poems
don't feel his pain but feel
a pain they really don't have,
that's not exactly real.

While whizzing around the track,
amusing our minds with art,
there circles the wind-up train
we call the human heart.

William Baer
Translated from the Spanish of
Miguel de Unamuno
1864 – 1936

Portugal

At the farthest edge of the Atlantic shore,
a barefoot and disheveled lady peers
into the waves, at the foot of the mountains, and hears
the distant, weeping pines. She sits before
the swirling sea, propping her head in her hands,
and like a lioness, fixes her gazing eyes
on the gateway of the sun, while the ocean cries
its tragic songs of wonders and distant lands.
It sings of tragedies and fate, while she,
with her feet in the foaming surf, dreams of history—
dreams of that once-great empire doomed to be,
so suddenly, lost and drowned in the gloomy sea—
then stares, through the mist, as the King of mystery,
Dom Sebastian, rises from the sea.

William Baer
Translated from the Latin of
Catullus
84 BC – 54 BC

Carmen CI

I've come across the nations and the seas,
beloved brother, to stand upon your grave,
to bring to you, at last, these gifts for the dead,
softly speaking, in vain, to your silent ashes.
The Fates have taken you away from me,
too soon, too premature, too unexpected.
Nevertheless, please accept these gifts,
in the tradition of our beloved forefathers,
as my tears rise again in my eyes and swell:
Goodbye, brother, forever—Hail and farewell!

Ned Balbo

Adapted from the French of

Charles Baudelaire

1821 – 1897

The Dispossessed

—A variation on Baudelaire's *"La Vie antérieure"*

I had it all. A mansion was my home—
seaside, of course: you should have seen the view,
waves crashing under cliffs, the sky deep blue
at dawn, sun-tinged and endless. Tiresome

with awe, guests wore me out, extolled my taste
in china, cellists, chattel, chef's preserves,
fine wine and art that everyone deserves
but I possessed. *Let everything they praised*

vanish for good! Take it!—but sense prevailed.
Time passed. . . . But on those days I woke in sun
and luxury, I looked past everyone

who labored for my profit yet recoiled
when I drew near, smiling: the squire they tended
dazzling, smug, and easily offended.

Ned Balbo

Adapted from the French of

Charles Baudelaire

1821 – 1897

Don Juan in Hell

—A variation on Baudelaire's *"Don Juan aux enfers"*

Don Juan, it's time. The caverns fill with light—
It's always dim light through which Charon rows,
the quiet water urging you through night
that lasts, and is, forever. Dangling toes

in dreadful waters, women watch from shore.
You knew them: some were suicides for you.
One waves, and smiles. How many nights before
you said you'd meet again—and now, it's true.

The servant, Sganarelle, you never paid
stands with your father, curiously calm,
now recompensed. They're undeceived and dead:
They see through every lie and stratagem

that served you in seduction or betrayal.
Your wife is waiting, too. Don't think she's stood
silent on shore, not sharing every detail—
And yet, to see you here calls back the flood

of hope, desire, and grief that we call Love. . . .
Is it from her you turn away, Don Juan,
or one who runs to greet you, sword in glove—
husband and knight, long-patient murdered man?

Ned Balbo
Adapted from the French of
Charles Baudelaire
1821 – 1897

Winter Bell

—A variation on Baudelaire's *"La Cloche fêlée"*

It's bittersweet on winter nights to listen
to a fire we're certain cannot last.
It twists and tears—but what fuel does it feed on?
Bells toll in fog. This fire contains the past—

Where does it go, set free? Church bells ring praise
to heaven and to anyone who hears,
though one bell's flawed, old veteran who'll raise
his voice to prove there's nothing that he fears.

I'm like that bell, but it's my soul that's flawed—
On nights so cold no sound could fill the void,
whatever cause it damns or celebrates,

my soul is mute, or worse: a cough that fades,
hopeless, half-heard beside a bloody lake
where dead men lie entangled, and I speak.

Tony Barnstone
Translated from the Greek of
C.P. Cavafy
1863 – 1933

Walls

"Τείχη"

With no compassion, pity, shame, they wrought
these massive walls around me, walls so high

I sit here and despair until the rot
consumes my thoughts: how poor my luck, how I

had many things I wished to do out there.
When they were building, how could I not hear?

I never heard the builders' racket, their
clangs, as they walled me up in here.

Translator's Note:

Cavafy worked as a clerk for thirty years in the Egyptian Ministry of Public Works, but had a second life as a gay poet at a time when this was dangerous, even life-threatening, and so a number of his poems suggest the secret life that he needed to keep behind "Walls"—or to keep secret through private circulation of the most erotic poems. "Walls" is a very unusual poem in that it is written in homophone rhymes.

—*Tony Barnstone*

Tony Barnstone
Translated from the Italian of
Francesco Petrarch
1304 – 1374

Sonnet 13

"Quando fra l'altre donne ad ora ad ora"

The lovely face of Love appears to me;
at times among the other girls it shows.
As much as they're less beautiful than she,
that much the love enamoring me grows.

I bless the planet, bless the time, the hour
that showed this height to which my vision lifts,
and to my spirit say: thank the power
that found you worthy to receive her gifts.

From her to me comes amorous thoughtfulness
that makes me wish to climb the virtuous heights,
makes me disdain what other men delights.

From her to me comes soulful loveliness,
a star illuminating Heaven's road,
so that I fly to her on wings of hope.

Tony Barnstone
Translated from the German of
Rainer Maria Rilke
1875 – 1926

The Panther

"Der Panther"

In the Jardin des Plantes, Paris

The bars pass by until his vision blurs
to nothing else but bars and bars again.
It is as if there were a thousand bars,
and past the thousand bars the world is gone.

His soft decisive striding is a force
that rotates in a circle's tiny maze.
It's like a ritual dance around a core
in which a once tremendous will stands dazed.

The curtains of the pupils do not part,
except at times—an image slipping in
runs electric through his tensile limbs—
then silently dies out inside the heart.

Tony Barnstone and *Bilal Shaw*
Translated from the Urdu of
Asadullah Khan Ghalib
1797 – 1869

Heaven's Teeth
"Ghazal 50"

How awful to see Heaven's teeth circling the finger
of those who deserved pearls to string their finger.

My souvenir of you is that you didn't give me one:
the day you left me you raised a ringless finger.

Asad, when I write hot words out of heartfire
no one can give the words I sing the finger.

Willis Barnstone

Translated from the Latin of

Horace

65 BC – 8 BC

Weathervane

Horace 1.5

Pyrrha,[1] what lean and perfumed boy
embraces you among the roses
    in a pleasant cave?
        Who has made you tie

your gold hair in simple elegance?
Yet he who now enjoys you will soon
    cry out against the
        ever-changing gods;

he will be stunned before the waters
shaken by the black winds. He who
    thinks you all golden
        and free of passion

---

1   Pyrrha means red or reddish in Greek, though here the woman's hair is gold-colored.

for another, ah, he does not know
the treacherous gales. Poor wretches
    before whom you seem
        untempted, shining!

The votive painting in the temple[2]
shows I have hung my dripping cloak
    before the fickle god,
        master of the sea.

---

2   It was common to hang a picture or other things in a shrine to celebrate or give thanks for an event. A sailor might hang a garment to Neptune, god of the sea.

Willis Barnstone
Translated from the Latin of
Horace
65 BC – 8 BC

Winter Breaking Up
Horace 4.7

Harsh winter breaks up with the good coming of spring
    and spring winds. Fishermen haul their dry hulls
down to the waters. Cattle are unhappy in their stables.
    So too the farmer by his fire. White frost is gone

from the meadows. Cytherean Venus[3] leads her dancers
    below the bold moon, and lovely Nymphs link arms
with Graces and dance on the earth while blazing Vulcan
    visits the forges of Cyclops the blacksmith.

Now is the time to loop your glowing hair with myrtle
    or blossoms issued by the loose earth.
Now in forest shadow it is right to sacrifice a burnt kid
    or lamb to Faunus, deity of the beasts.

---

3   Cythera (Kythera) is a Greek island in the Adriatic Sea, off the southwest coast of the Greek mainland where Venus is said to have been born. More often Venus as Aphrodite (the foam-born) is said to have been born in waters off the city of Paphos on the southern coast of Cyprus.

Pale death is walking, knocking at a poor man's cottage
    or a prince's palace. O lucky handsome Sestius,
life's brief span forbids us from having long hope.
    Soon the night of phantoms will seize you

and will hold you in Pluto's cheerless hall. When you
    are there, the dice won't choose you lord
of the feast or let you gaze with wonder at tender Lycidas
    whom all young men and virgins desire.

Willis Barnstone
Translated from the Latin of
Horace
65 BC – 8 BC

Cold Winter

    Horace 1.9

    See how the Soracte[4] mountain glistens
    in the snow, how the struggling forests
        can no longer hold up
            their burdens, and the streams

    have stiffened into ice in the acute cold.
    Melt the frost by piling many logs on the fire
        and generously open the Sabine[5]
            jars with fourth-year wine,

    O Thaliarche.[6] Leave the rest to the gods,
    who once they have quieted the winds
        battering the boiling sea,
            the cypresses and old ash trees

---

4   A mountain of three thousand feet located west of the river Tiber.
5   The reference is to Horace's villa near Rome and the greater Tivoli (Tibur) region. A tribe called the Sabines once inhabited that region.
6   Greek for "ruler of the feast."

will no longer shiver. Forget tomorrow,
and every day use what chance dreams up.
    And while young, don't neglect
        sweet love and dancing;

old brooding age is still remote. Arrange
for your encounters in the market squares
    at the hour of whispers below
        the night. A young woman's

laughter is hiding in a remote corner.
As for those ornaments ripped off her arm
    and finger, she sees them gone
        and barely feigns resistance.

Willis Barnstone
Translated from the Latin of
Horace
65 BC – 8 BC

Enjoy the Day
Horace 1.11

To know is wrong. Leuconaë.[7] Don't ask what end the gods
    have determined for you and me.
Don't be tempted by the Babylonian astrological charts
    to know the nature of our trials.[8]

Better to endure whatever comes whether Jupiter gives us
    many winters or only this last one
which is weakening the cliffs along the Tyrrhenian Sea.[9]
    Be wise. Strain the wine clear,

for the space of life is brief and makes long hope short.
    Even now as we are talking,
jealous time escapes. Hang on to day, *carpe diem*,[10]
    and don't believe tomorrow.

---

[7] From the Greek for white- or light-complexioned.
[8] The calculations of the Chaldaean (Babylonian) astrologers foretold the future.
[9] The sea from western Italy to Sicily, Sardinia, and Corsica.
[10] Seize the day.

Willis Barnstone
Translated from the Latin of
Horace
65 BC – 8 BC

O Ship, The Waves Are Sweeping You[11]
Horace 1.14

O ship, the waves are sweeping you out to sea
again. What are you up to! Break your back
    to make port! Can't you see,
        on one side your oars are lost,

wild African[12] gales have split your mast,
your yardarms groan, and with ropes gone
    your keel won't last long
        against the hurtling implacable

waters. Your sails are in shreds, your onboard
tiny gods have sunk, and no one hears your cry.
    Though your Black Sea[13] pine hull
        is a daughter of noble forest timber,

---

11   Ode 1.14, often called The Ship of State ode. Here Horace imitates the ship of state poems of Alkaios of Lesbos (Alceus), who used the ship in dangerous waters as an extended metaphor to depict the perils of the state. A celebrated American poem that follows the metaphor of the classical ship of state model is Walt Whitman's "O Captain, My Captain" in which the perils of the state are recounted after its captain, Abraham Lincoln, lies on the deck, assassinated.

12   Southwest winds, traditionally from Carthage.

13   *Pontic,* from *pontos,* Greek for sea, as in Hellespont. Pontos here refers to a region of eastern ancient Greece noted for its excellent ship timber. It is now part of northern Turkey.

bragging about its name and genesis
is hopeless. A scared sailor can't rely
　　on a painted stern. Be careful
　　　　not to be the wind's toy.

Once my worry and tedious pain, now
I beg you, my love, to sail clear of the lane
　　of waters raging among
　　　　the luminous Cyclades.[14]

14　　Cyclades: white glittering islands in the Aegean Sea. Ferocious winds blow especially in summer around the Cyclades, a phenomenon first described in Homer's *Odyssey*.

Willis Barnstone

Translated from the Latin of

Horace

65 BC – 8 BC

Invitation

    Horace 1.23

Chloë,[15] you run from me like a young deer
seeking a fearful mother through bleak hills,
    yet you are wrong to fear
        the forest and the winds.

The deer's heart and thighs begin to tremble
should a brief leaf quiver in the wind
    or a green lizard graze
        against a bramble bush.

But dear Chloë, I do not wish to crush you
like a savage tiger, a Gaetulian lion.[16]
    Only give up your mother
        and come, ripe, to a man.

---

15   Chloë means "a tender or new shoot" in Greek.
16   The Gaetulians were a people of ancient Morocco.

Willis Barnstone

Translated from the Latin of

Horace

65 BC – 8 BC

Highhanded Matchmaking

Horace 1.33

Albius, do not mope over Glycera,
sing no sad endless elegies for her
nor question why a youth outshines you
    or why she broke her vows.

Lovely Lycoris of the low forehead[17]
burns for Cyrus; Cyrus is rebuffed
by cold Pholoë who would sooner lie
    with an Apulian[18] wolf

than sleep with such a common lover.
Such is the doing of Venus who loves
to lure hostile bodies and hearts
    under her brassy yoke.

---

17   A low or narrow forehead was an admired feature. In Ode 1.7.26 Horace laments his own receding hairline.
18   Apula, modern Puglia in southern Italy, was Horace's province.

When a worthier passion called me,
I was sweetly enchained by slave-born
Myrtale stormier than Hadrian waves
    rounding Calabria's gulf.[19]

---

19   The poem is thought to be addressed to the Latin poet Albius Tibullus.

Willis Barnstone
Translated from the Latin of
Horace
65 BC – 8 BC

Cleopatra

Horace 1.37

Now for drinking, now for hitting the earth
and dancing, leaping, now, friends, is the time,
    for a Salian[20] feast to decorate
        the couches of the gods.

Before now it would have been wrong
to bring out Caecuban[21] wine from ancient bins
    while the mad queen plotted the ruin
        and funeral of Rome and empire

with her sick gang of ugly infected men
drunk on impotent hope and fortune's
    cheap candies. But by the escape
        of scarcely any ship from fire[22]

---

20   Salian priests of the god Mars were known for their lavish banquets and their leaping dances.
21   An excellent wine from Latium.
22   Antony and Cleopatra's defeat at Actium in 31 BC was surely not of 300 ships as Octavius Caesar (later the Emperor Augustus) claimed. A century later Plutarch suggests that Cleopatra contemplated hauling her remaining ships overland to the Red Sea, with all her wealth, and sailing away to found a new empire.

Caesar sobered her mind from the madness
of Mareotic[23] wine and she came into
>   true terror as his galleys
>   > picked up speed and she fled

from Italy as if a hawk chased a soft dove
or a quick hunter closed in on a hare
>   over snow plains of Haemonia[24]
>   > with the end of chaining

a deadly monster. But she wanted a nobler
death. She had no womanly fear of a sword,
>   nor tried to speed her fleet
>   > to a secret harbor.

Serene, she bravely gazed at her fallen palace,
she bravely picked up the poisonous snake
>   and held it to her body to drink
>   > its black venom,

growing increasingly fierce in her deliberate death.
No humble woman before his glorious triumph,[25]
>   she would not be carried off
>   > unqueened on small hostile ships.[26]

---

23 Potent wine from Marea, a city by a lake of the same name, south of Alexandria.
24 A hunting region in northern Thessaly.
25 Cleopatra abhorred the idea of being paraded live and disgraced in Caesar's formal triumph march. In August 29 her effigy was paraded in Rome.
26 Horace called the hostile light galleys Liburnians. The poem reveals a progression from an initial denigration of Cleopatra and her cohorts to complete admiration for the queen's fearless serenity and pride before her determined death.

Mark S. Bauer
Translated from the Latin of
Martial
c. 40 – c. 103

Martial II:53

Be free, my friend? You're whistling in the dark.

But if you're serious, this life's no lark:

Eat out? Forget your favorite restaurants.

Bordeaux and ports? As gone as your old haunts.

Home furnishing high marks? Put up with partials.

New clothes? Try Syms or TJ Maxx or Marshall's.

And social life? Cheap dates for you, at best

(though you'll live well with those who pass this test).

Now for the toughest trade, if you've the will:

Your corner office for a cubicle.

Choose these—which to your world seem dire straits—

And you'll live life far freer than Bill Gates.

Mark S. Bauer
Translated from the Latin of
Martial
c. 40 – c. 103

Parcere personis, dicere devitiis
after "Martial X:33"

You say at times my lines condemn,

pressing a point *ad hominem*.

I beg that you remember when

I wield what seems a poison pen

it's not to launch some vengeful plan:

I sing of arms, not of the man.

Michael Bradburn-Ruster
Translated from the Spanish of
José Luis Puerto
b. 1953

The House
"La casa"

> Stone by stone, I endure
> My house's demolition
> —René Char

The house was the first space
Of which I was deprived.
There, the mark of exile was made present.
Of the primordial place I was stripped
And now when I utter
Little convent, bay tree,
Garden plot, country house,
Living room, kitchen, stepladder, bedroom,
Cherry tree by the river,
My voice expresses to the air the wounds
Inscribed in absence's calligraphy.
Later, other ambits
Were to embrace my existence in space,
Yet none was the cipher
Of the primordial place given me
To inhabit the world.

Today it's gone, that house

That harbored me on earth,

That received my breath's initiation;

Only the pilgrimage from place to place,

And a space in the light of memory

That gives meaning to the world and saves us:

The primordial place,

The house that was kingdom,

My speech is made of exile from that place.

When one has come to know

The indelible space of the garden,

A life is spent searching

To find it once again.

—from *Sílabas del Mundo* [Syllables of the World]

Michael Bradburn-Ruster
Translated from the Spanish of
José Luis Puerto
b. 1953

Chestnut Tree

"Tú,/ En esa vida"

You,
In that life
Above.
Always in that stillness
Where you disclose yourself.
In that here which I see and cannot reach.
Always in that silence
Asking nothing ever but to abide
And thus be nudity,
Leaves, flowers and fruits. So that you remain
Solace and peace for one who gazes. Tree,
Brother with whom I dream
Of some day mingling

from *Señales* [Traces]

Heidi Czerwiec and **Claudia Routon**
Translated from the Spanish of
José Corredor-Matheos
b. 1929

Before a painting by Jordi Pallarés

*"Ante un cuadro de
Jordi Pallarés"*

The selfsame light that inflames
the yellows of a sun
that will never flicker out
illuminates your blacks,
which reveal
that there, where there is nothing,
everything gleams.
Your reds horrify us,
for we witness ourselves
split open
across your canvases,
after the sacrifice.
Pictures such as yours
can cause trembling

in one who doesn't know
that to paint is to feel
the harsh shudder
of pure beauty.

—from *Un pez que va por el jardín* [A Fish Who Wanders through the Garden]

Heidi Czerwiec and *Claudia Routon*
Translated from the Spanish of
José Corredor-Matheos
b. 1929

Before a still life by Juan van der Hamen

"Ante un bodegón de
Juan van der Hamen"

The sparkle of crystal.
Mortal splendor
stems from the flowers.
A few foolish cherries
and shy artichokes.
You breathe in perfumes.
You hear melody
beyond music.
You know what these images
embody but not
the reason for
their splendor.
And you name your feeling
with a word—
always a forgery.

—from *Un pez que va por el jardín* [A Fish Who Wanders through the Garden]

Heidi Czerwiec and **Claudia Routon**
Translated from the Spanish of
José Corredor-Matheos
b. 1929

Before a painting by Marc Rothko

> *"Ante un cuadro
> de Marc Rothko"*

Marc Rothko knows how to see
things as they are:
disembodied radiance,
color lively at the borders
of shadows.
He takes the paintbrush and lets
red burn,
blue paint the breeze,
green grow and ochre
eddy,
how white melds
all colors
or how jet black rejects them.
Impermanent paint,
pure spirit,
mirror of the void,

where I recognize myself.
Being clearly aware
that nothing in the nothing
sustains itself
makes this beauty
even more dazzling.

—from *Un pez que va por el jardín* [A Fish Who Wanders through the Garden]

Brett Foster
Translated from the Italian of
Cecco Angiolieri
c. 1260 – c. 1312

Hedging My Bets

"I' potre' anzi ritornare in ieri"

    Odds are better to return to yesterday
and find Becchina's affection all restored,
or grind a diamond into finest flour,
or see some friars accept the pauper's way,
    or grow a potbelly like Mino Pieri,
or happily suck on a chicken foot,
than for extended fever to take him out—
that devil called the elder Angiolieri.
    For if either Galen or Hippocrates
were living, each could diagnose (or try)
my father less surely than Donatus,
    that grammar guy. So how could this man die,
who knows what's what, whose constitution's thus,
who like an ostrich can digest iron straight?

Brett Foster
Translated from the Italian of
Cecco Angiolieri
c. 1260 – c. 1312

The Marriage of Rope and Roof Beam

"Quand'i' solev'udir ch'un fiorentino"

    Those times when I would hear a Florentine
had grown so desperate from his great pain
that hanging himself became a certainty,
I thought God had fashioned an uncanny thing.
    Now it seems a more predictable reaction
than for a marble-cutter, who for progress' sake
has worked his saw all day without a break,
to take a cup of wine and knock it back.
    Because I've known firsthand such sorrow, hope's
absence convinces me that deadly pain
would be a hundred thousand times more bearable.
    That this anguish is as strong and terrible
as my sonnet says, and more by twice again,
I'll demonstrate with less than two ropes.

Brett Foster
Translated from the Italian of
Cecco Angiolieri
c. 1260 – c. 1312

See You, Wouldn't Want to Be You

"I' non vi miro perzar, morditori"

    Your slanders will not faze me, cannibals,
that I'll fall back again and share your state.
Daily your colors change, a thousand in all,
before your stolen cash is calculated.

    Did you actually believe it, gentle sirs,
that since I gambled all in search of thrills
I'd have to take the vow of minor friars,
no longer finger coins or larger bills?

    But here's enough to make your heart explode:
I've so maneuvered to have smoothly thrived,
with places here in town and down the road.

    And best of all (it's really sweet to me)—
to see you, each of you, die of jealousy
since you must trick and swindle to survive.

Catherine Chandler

Translated from the Spanish of
Delmira Agustini
1886 – 1914

My Loves

"Mis amores"

Today they have returned.
By every path of the night they have come
To weep in my bed.
There were, there are, so many of them!
I do not know which ones are living or if any have died.
In order to mourn them all, I will mourn myself.
The night soaks up my sobs
Like a black handkerchief.

There are sun-gilded heads, as if ripened . . .
There are heads weakened by darkness and mystery,
Heads crowned with an invisible thorn,
Heads blushing from rose-colored dreams,
Heads that yield to the cushions of hell,
Heads that would rather rest in heaven,
Some that never smell of springtime,
And many that smack of winter flowers.

All those heads torment me like sores . . .
They hurt me like the dead . . .
Oh! . . . and the eyes . . . the eyes hurt me even more: they are deceitful . . .
Undefined, green, grey, blue, black,
They burn and they glow,
They are caresses, pain, constellation, hell.
On all their light, on all their flames,
My soul was set afire and my body was readied.
They made me thirst for all those mouths . . .
For all those mouths that bloom in my bed;
Red or pale glasses of honey or bitterness,
With irises of harmony or roses of silence,
I drank life from all these glasses,
I drink death from all these glasses . . .
The poisonous, intoxicating garden of their mouths
Where their souls and bodies breathed,
Drunk with tears,
Has encircled my bed . . .

And the hands, the hands full of secret
Destinies and spread out with rings of mystery . . .
There are hands that were born with kid gloves;
Hands that overflow with the flowers of desire,
Hands in which one feels an invisible dagger,
And hands in which one sees an intangible scepter;
Pale or dark, sensual or strong,
They can all entangle a dream.
With sadness of soul,
The bodies surrender

Unshrouded, saintly
Dressed in desire.
Magnets of my arms
Honeycombs of my heart
Bend over my bed as if toward an invisible abyss . . .

Oh, I have sought your hands among all the hands!
Your mouth among the mouths, your body among the bodies,
Of all the heads I want your head,
Of all those eyes, I want only your eyes!
You are the saddest, for being the most loved,
You have arrived first for having come the farthest . . .

Oh, the dark head I have never touched
And the light pupils that I gazed on for so long!
The dark-circled eyes the evening and I recklessly made even deeper,
The strange pallor I yielded to unknowingly,
Come to me: mind to mind;
Come to me: body to body
You will tell me what you have done with my first breath,
You will tell me what you have done with the dream of that kiss.
We will say whether we are weeping to find ourselves alone . . .
You will tell me if you have died,
My sorrow will slowly dress the bedroom in mourning
And I will embrace your shadow until my body dies,
And in the deep silence of darkness,
And in the deep darkness of silence,
Weeping, weeping even as we die, we will keep vigil over
Our son: memory.

Translator's Note:

Delmira Agustini was born on October 24, 1886, in Montevideo, Uruguay. This poem was written not long before Agustini's ex-husband and still secret lover, Enrique Job Reyes, shot her to death before committing suicide on July 6, 1914.

Three versions of "Mis amores" display important variations, addressed in various ways by scholars dedicated to establishing the definitive version of the poem.

Alejandro Cáceres, an associate professor of Spanish at the Department of Foreign Languages and Literatures at Southern Illinois University Carbondale, Agustini scholar and editor of a critical edition of Agustini's complete poems (Ediciones de la Plaza, Montevideo, 1999) chose to use the version of "Mis amores" published posthumously in *Obras completas. El Rosario de Eros.* (Ediciones Maximino García. Montevideo: *El Siglo Ilustrado,* 1924). In his Preface, Cáceres admits that he is not a native English speaker and that he relied on a research assistant with a BA in classics ("with fluency in Spanish") as his translation consultant. The result is a competent though greatly flawed translation.

Magdalena García Pinto's *Delmira Agustini. Poesías completas* (Ediciones Cátedra, Madrid, 2006), on the other hand, uses the text from Agustini's manuscripts in the Biblioteca Nacional de Montevideo. Footnotes indicate that, based on this source, García Pinto believes the poet had not yet finished revising the poem, and that the 1924 text of "Mis amores" was based on one of two versions transcribed and "corrected" by Agustini's father, Santiago, under the family's supervision. García Pinto opts for Agustini's handwritten manuscript version, which Carina Blixen, in her *Poesía—Delmira Agustini* (Ediciones del Pizarrón, Montevideo, 2000), describes as "muy corregido, tachado, sobreescrito" (full of corrections, erasures, and overwritings).

The differences consist of a few words in lines 20, 33, 34, and 36, minor differences in formatting such as stanza breaks and indentations, and punctuation discrepancies such as commas, periods, additional ellipses and exclamation points in the 1924 version.

The two most striking differences occur, first, in line 64, where the entire line in the 1924 version reads in the second person singular, whereas in Agustini's manuscript, the line appears in the first person plural, altering both tone and meaning. The second major difference is found in the repetition of the phrase "Si has muerto," between lines 65 and 66 in the 1924 version. In Agustini's manuscript, that phrase appears only once, in line 65.

I have chosen to translate the version that appears both in García Pinto and Blixen, i.e., Agustini's (perhaps not final) version and hope that this new translation will better reflect the depth and beauty of the original.

My husband, Victor Hugo Oliveira, is Uruguayan and we reside part of every year in Uruguay.

—*Catherine Chandler*

Terese Coe
Translated from the German of
Heinrich Heine
1797 – 1856

Happiness

"Nicht lange täuschte mich das Glück"

The happiness that you conferred
so briefly worked its art,
your picture like a hollow dream
that dragged me by the heart.

The light of dawn, the burning sun
came up, the fog departed;
and we had long since made an end
of what we had not started.

Maryann Corbett
Translated from the French of
Christine de Pizan
1364 – c. 1430

Ballade IV from *Les Cent Ballades*

By envy, which upends the world's designs,
treason is fed in secret, in the hearts
of wicked men. The ferment in their minds
nourishes in their deeds the trickster's arts
through which they bring about their evil ends.
From these they wring out gain in all its forms
by treachery, and not by deeds of arms.

Troy was a power, once upon a time,
grand beyond every citadel and court,
reigning above the world, and in its prime
the flowering of nobility's high art.
But then the Greeks prevailed, and Troy was burnt,
and Trojans were made slaves. The victor's terms
were set by trickery, not by deeds of arms.

And Alexander, all the earth his prize,
was thus betrayed; another treacherous dart
pierced Arthur (who in fairyland now lies,
they say) when Mordred's evil broke his heart.
Achilles, when he dealt a deadly hurt
to Hector whom all nobleness adorns,
won out by treason, not by deeds of arms.

This is not mockery, Prince: I speak my mind.
Be on your guard for madness of this kind!
See, if you can, how grievous are the harms
when treachery takes the place of deeds of arms.

Maryann Corbett
Translated from the French of
Christine de Pizan
1364 – c. 1430

Ballade VII from *Les Cent Ballades*

Ah, wretched Fortune! How you've thrust
me down, so low now, once so high!
Your venom-pointed arrows press
my heart to grave uncertainty.
No other harm of yours, no force
could do a crueler injury
than this: to steal the loving ease
that kept my life a joy to me.

I was so wholly happy once
I thought no one on earth could be
more fortune-favored than I was.
I went on living fearlessly,
believing it was powerless,
that miserable jealousy
of yours, which stole the loving ease
that kept my life a joy to me.

Fearsome, changeable, shadow-crossed,
you struck me down too violently.
Your envious malice cast the curse
that raised these mounds of misery.
Could you not settle scores, alas,
by any means less merciless
than snatching from me love and ease
that kept my life a joy to me?

Most gentle Prince, I ask: Was this
not evil, spiteful cruelty
to rob me of the loving ease
that kept my life a joy to me?

Maryann Corbett

Translated from the French of

Christine de Pizan

1364 – c. 1430

Ballade LIX from *Les Cent Ballades*

I watch them come and go, those fashionable
lovers, across the abbey naves and aisles,
young men who dare not breathe a syllable
to their beloved ladies, lest the wiles
of gossips hound them, sniffing at new styles
in slander. So to church, to gaze, they go.
And when they leave the church masked in their smiles,
are their hearts eased? I think the answer's no.

And if this does them any good at all,
it's dearly bought, that walk across the tile.
For they who keep the courtly lover's rule
take up a cause that soon becomes a trial.
Love keeps them underdogs, cringing and vile,
fearful to let a bit of scandal show.
Whether their worth is one coin or a pile,
are their hearts eased? I think the answer's no.

It isn't wise to mix with shady people.
They get no good, no ill, from courtly style
in loving—only hindrance, not the mettle
to speed things. Their deception's black as bile.
They're subtle. Shifty. Every move is guile.
And are they truly loved? They hardly know
or care. Does such weak taste for what's worthwhile
ease their poor hearts? I think the answer's no.

Maryann Corbett
Translated from the French of
Christine de Pizan
1364 – c. 1430

Ballade LXXXVI from *Les Cent Ballades*

In times we read about in myths,
Olympian gods and goddesses
observed Love's dictates, Ovid says.
From love there followed great distress:
the loyalty, the promises
to keep, the undeceiving speech—
if truth is what the fables teach.

Down from the heavens' height of bliss
they leaned, despite their loftiness,
to learn what being a lover is.
Neglecting wealth, hanging expense,
those all-exalted deities
risked everything—all they were worth—
if poets' fables tell the truth.

Thus were they constrained to please
nymphets and enchantresses.
The rulers of the gods were these:
satyrettes and mistresses
in love, to whom in wild excess
they gave their bodies, and goods too,
if what the fables say is true.

Ergo: A prince, or a princess
should be prepared to study well
what proper objects love should bless,
if we believe what fables tell.

Dick Davis
Translated from the Persian

Five Poems by Women Writing in Persian
17th – 19th century

Nur Jahan (the wife of Jahangir) 17th century

> They say that with a gentle breeze
> > the petals of a rose-bud part;
> A smile from my belovèd is
> > the key that will unlock my heart.

★ ★ ★

Jahan Khanom, mother of Nasraddinshah, 19th century

> A man or woman who is wise will be
> Honored in every place and company—
> A man or woman who knows nothing shows
> That he or she's a thorn without a rose.

★ ★ ★

Ayesheh-ye afghan, 18th / 19th century

> I saw the sunset in the sky
> > at evening prayer time, tulip red—
> It was as though they'd killed the sun
> > And there her blood-soaked skirts were spread.

★ ★ ★

Ayesheh-ye afghan, 18th / 19th century

    My Love was here; but there was no one here, that day;
    Kindly His strong grip snatched my wounded heart away—

    And when the One who stole my heart unveiled His face
    The angels and mankind knelt down before such Grace.

    I slept, and in my dream a flower-filled garden shone;
    I started up from sleep—all trace of it was gone.

    That day, I handed Him my vow of slavery;
    The pens of angel scribes recorded it for me.

★ ★ ★

Reshheh, 18th / 19th century

    I've put up with a lifetime of your tyranny
                            hoping for your fidelity,
    And now my life's gone by, and faithfulness from you
                            was never once vouchsafed to me.

    From all the world I chose you, and now see
                             what recompense was given me—
    It's that I hear the scorn and blame of all the world
                            deriding and reviling me.

And if it's true that handsome lovers' promises
                               are weak and broken easily
I've never seen or heard, my love, of any vow
                               as weak as that you made to me.

My stony-hearted love, you broke my heart, but I've
                               kept faith with you unceasingly
And I have never taken back my love for you,
                               even though you've abandoned me.

You pierced me with the arrow of your callousness
                               while I lay weeping piteously—
What was my sin but this, that I put up with all
                               your cold hardheartedness to me?

And since I drank the wine of your first kindness down
                               it's never happened that I see
My glass of pleasure empty of that poisoned drink
                               my loving you has poured for me.

And what has Reshheh gained from all the benefits
                               his cloud of gifts has poured on me,
Now that the lightning of my grief has burned
                               the fields I planted once so hopefully?

Adam Elgar
Translated from the Italian of
Gaspara Stampa
1523 – 1554

Rime 4

"Quando fu prima il mio signor concetto"

When first the seed that made my lord was sown
the stars and planets gave him every grace
and all the gifts that crown the human race
so that perfection might be his alone.
Saturn endowed him with a lofty mind;
from Jove he learned to seek what's right and fair;
Mars made him every enemy's despair;
Phoebus brought style and made his thoughts refined;

From Venus came his beauty's perfect form;
from Mercury his eloquence: a shame
the Moon brought coldness. I'd prefer him warm.
Such rare, fine qualities; and each of these
sets me ablaze with my fierce, brilliant flame,
while all it took was one to make him freeze.

Adam Elgar

Translated from the Italian of

Gaspara Stampa

1523 – 1554

Rime 5

"Io assimiglio il mio signor al cielo"

My lord is like the sky, it seems to me.
I see the sunshine in his lovely face;
his eyes are stars; his speech is of such grace
it's like divine Apollo's harmony.
Downpours and frosts, and thunderclaps and hail
are indignation, when his anger stirs;
calm seas and Zephyrs come when he prefers
kindly to tear away his rage's veil.

He's like the springtime and the blooms of May
when promising the honor of his care;
that's when my hope can blossom like a flower.
It's dreadful winter when his mood turns sour
with threats to change his mind and move elsewhere,
so all my rich gifts would be stripped away.

Adam Elgar

Translated from the Italian of

Gaspara Stampa

1523 – 1554

Rime 8

"Se, cosí come sono abietta e vile"

If, though I am a woman vile and low,
I bear within me such a noble flame,
why can't I be permitted to proclaim
this with so style and brio, even so?
If Love, playing a new, unheard-of game,
has thrown me higher than I'd ever go,
may he not strike another novel blow
and make my pain and pen one and the same?

He'll have to do it through a miracle
if he cannot achieve it naturally,
by making nature metaphysical.
How? That I cannot say explicitly,
but with my fortunes at their pinnacle,
I feel new style imprinted onto me.

Adam Elgar
Translated from the Italian of
Gaspara Stampa
1523 – 1554

Rime 21

"S'io, che son dio, ed ho meco tant'armi"

"Though I'm a god with such a mighty bow
and arrows, your lord makes me second best,
for his new beauty is the loveliest,
always *en garde* to deal me one more blow;
so is it possible that I would know
a way to help you in your hopeless quest
to thaw the ice, his heart's unwelcome guest,
by prayer, advice, or song? The answer's no.

Your only hope's the passing of the years,
or some good fortune; I've no other way
to show you till a better one appears."
He says these words, and then he flies away,
leaving me here to shed my bitter tears,
and wail at my misfortune night and day.

Adam Elgar
Translated from the Italian of
Gaspara Stampa
1523 – 1554

Rime 31

"Chi non sa come dolce il cor si fura"

Someone whose heart has never flown away
in sweetness, who's not felt his passion's fire
quenched sweetly and the ache of his desire
sweetly allayed, his soul freed from dismay,
should come just once, my lord, to hear you sing,
and know he is exceptionally blest
because your lovely voice enchants to rest
the earth, the sky, and every living thing.

Hearing your spirit speak, he'll see the air
becoming limpid, and imperious
winds, storms and waters cease to roar and blare.
And when you've made the world harmonious
he'll well believe a tiger, snake and bear
were spellbound by the song of Orpheus.

Andrew Frisardi
Translated from the Italian of
Dante Alighieri
1265 – 1321

"*Amor che ne la mente mi ragiona*"

Lord Love, who talks and reasons[27] in my mind
about my lady so desirously,[28]
moves things[29] that have to do with her, in me,
through which my intellect then goes astray.
His speaking always makes so sweet a sound,
the soul which listens to and feels that source
says: "Oh, alas! I do not have such force
that what I hear about her I can say."
And surely I must leave off right away—
if I desire to write the things I hear
about her—what my intellect can't grasp,
and most of what it has
known too, since how to say it isn't clear.
So, if my rhymes are marred by some defect

---

27   I use two verbs to translate the one *"ragiona,"* and not simply to fill up the ten syllables of the line. *Ragionare* often does mean "to converse" or "to discuss," but the root of the word cannot be ignored—it is no accident that Dante pairs *ragione*, reason, with *Amor*, Love, since the alchemical marriage of the two is a central theme not only of this poem but of Dante's entire oeuvre.

28   "Desirously" is *disiosamente* in Dante's poem. In the *Divine Comedy*, too, Dante will often use adverbs ending with *-mente* (the Italian equivalent of our *-ly* adverbs) to slow a verse down for emotional emphasis.

29   Dante likes the word *cosa/cose* (sg. and pl. for "things") a lot, using it over four hundred times in the *Convivio* alone. He doesn't specify what, precisely, because these "things" (qualities, wonders, attractions) are mysterious. He doesn't know quite what they are so he uses the generic word.

when they set out upon their praise of her,
just blame it on the feeble intellect,
and on our speech, whose strength is not enough
to tell of everything that's said by Love.

The sun[30] sees nothing, as he circles all
the world, nobler than at the hour he gives
his light to that part where the woman lives
about whom Love has made me write and speak.
In heaven, she holds each Intellect in thrall,
and people here below[31] in love discover
that she is in their thoughts as well whenever
Love gives something to them of her peace.
Her being, to the One who gives it lease,
is so pleasing that all his powers stream
into her always past our nature's claims.[32]
Her pure soul,[33] which obtains
from him this boon and wholeness, is then keen
to make it manifest in what she guides;
for in her loveliness such things are seen,
the eyes of all those people where she shines[34]

---

30   As often in Dante, a transparent symbol for God—as he explicitly states in the *Convivio*'s commentary on this poem.
31   People here on earth, such as Dante himself, specifically any lover of wisdom, i.e., philosopher in the etymological sense.
32   The miraculous power of truth or wisdom transcends ordinary or ego-bound thought.
33   The soul or form (in the Aristotelian sense) of philosophy is love.
34   The soul that receives this blessing from God shines in the eyes of lovers of wisdom, or sages and seers, who in turn, because of the light they transmit, make those who look into their eyes fall in love just as they have. (We might recall the description in Plato's *Ion* of the transmission of poetic inspiration from poet to minstrel or bard to audience—all on a continuum united by the power of the Muse.) The images in this passage are all micro stages of the emanationist theology (a theory of "descent" from the divine principle into manifestation/creation) that permeates this poem, and especially this stanza.

send envoys to the heart full of desires,
which take on air and then turn into sighs.

In her, celestial potency descends
as in an angel who beholds it; let
that woman who does not believe this yet
be with her and see what her actions show.
Here on earth, each time she speaks, there bends
a spirit down from heaven, one that stresses
that the lofty virtue she possesses
surpasses what is rightly ours to know.
The lovely acts she shows to people go
calling on Love, each vying with the other
in a voice that makes him feel its weight.
About her we can state:
noble in woman is what's found in her,
and beauty is but her similitude.
And we can say her face helps us aver
that wonder has become our certitude;
so that our faith is all but guaranteed:
thus from eternity she was decreed.

And in her face appear things that reflect
the beauties and delights of paradise:
I mean in her sweet smile and in her eyes,[35]
where Love, as if he's home, conveys them to:
such things as overwhelm our intellect
as does a ray of sun to feeble sight.

---

35   The pleasures or beauties that appear in her eyes and smile are manifestations of love, if not the actual presence of Love—an incarnation of Amor-Love, in fact.

And since I cannot gaze on them outright,
I have to keep my words about them few.
Her beauty rains small flames of fire, imbued
with an animating noble spirit's grace,[36]
the true creator of all virtuous thought,
which thunderclap to naught
the inborn vices that make people base.
Let any woman sensing that some feel
her beauty lacks a peaceful, humble face,
watch her who is humility's ideal!
She is the one who humbles the perverse;[37]
He thought of her Who moved the universe.

Canzone, what you say is opposite,
it seems, to what a sister[38] of yours states:
the woman who's so humble by your lights,
she claims is heartless and contemptuous.
You know the sky is always limpid, lit,
and never really in itself goes dark,
although our eyes for many reasons mark
that stars from time to time seem tenebrous.
So, when she says she's supercilious,
she sees her not by truth, but by how she
saw only what appearances declared;
for once the soul was scared,

---

36 In the *Convivio* Dante says this noble spirit is the *"diritto appetito,"* the desire for the good, for virtue—desire ennobled, in short.
37 *"Perverso"*: Dante interprets this etymologically, as "turned away"—i.e., all who are turned away from the true and the beautiful.
38 The ballad *Voi che savete ragionar d'Amore;* see my comments about this stanza in the "Translator's Note" on page 64.

and is so still, so that the things I see
whenever she's aware of me seem cruel.
In this way ask for pardon, if need be;
and when you can, and go before her, you'll
say: "Lady, may you be pleased: if you are,
I'm going to talk about you near and far."

Translator's Note:

Amor che ne la mente mi ragiona (composed c. 1295) is Dante's great allegorical canzone about the love of wisdom—of the marriage of love (or, in medieval thought, will) and intellect (or knowledge). Under the influence of Boethius and Solomon's sapiential writings in the Bible—and incorporating stock imagery from the courtly love poetry he had mastered—Dante personifies philosophy as a beautiful and wise woman: Lady Philosophy.

    This is the second of three canzones in Dante's unfinished philosophical treatise the *Convivio* (c. 1304 – 7), where he interprets this and the other canzoni allegorically. Dante famously refers to *Amor che ne la mente* in *Purgatorio* II, where he requests of his friend the musician Casella, newly arrived on the island of Mount Purgatory, that he sing it to him as consolation for the darkness and trial of the inferno-journey Dante has just completed. Also well known, among scholars, is the idea that the episode in *Purgatorio* is Dante's palinode of his earlier philosophical phase, epitomized in this poem. Certainly, the guardian of purgatory-arrivals, Cato, will brook no loitering on the part of Dante and Virgil, Casella, and the other purgatorial souls entranced by Casella's singing and Dante's poem. The suggestion may be that philosophy is just a stage on the journey to the truth as such, which is God; or that art for art's sake—the trance of the poem—is itself a trap or diversion from the spirit's ultimate quest.

    Stanza 1, as D. himself states in the *Convivio*, is a proem to the canzone. It is a statement of the ineffableness of love, and especially of the love of wisdom, for which there are two causes: the limitations of our understanding and the limitations of our speech, of what language can do. The final stanza is a conventional envoy that sends the canzone (personified and directly addressed) off into the world; but it is also a justification or explanation on Dante's part for an apparent contradiction between this poem and his earlier ballad *Voi che savete ragionar d'Amore* [All you who know how to discuss Love], which describes the heroine of this poem in very different terms, as *"disdegnosa,"* or haughty-contemptuous, and *"fera,"* or cruel. The middle three stanzas of the present poem are the heart of its content. They begin with a depiction of celestial attraction or influx vis-à-vis Lady Philosophy, which then, within a single stanza (2), is followed in its descent into the lovers of Wisdom, philosophers, who receive the impulse that originates in heaven and finally issues as light in the eyes of the wise and sighs from those whom the wise inspire (see the closing lines of stanza 2). The "Intellects" at the opening of stanza 2 are the "angelic" or celestial intelligences—metaphysical intermediaries between God and the creation. Dante says in *Convivio* that Lady Philosophy is praised in her entirety in this stanza 2, while stanza 3 is dedicated to her soul and stanza 4 to her body.

Several critics have opined that his canzone was not originally allegorical, but was written about Dante's love for an actual woman and was rationalized later; although the general consensus now is that this, among some other lyrics that Dante wrote in the 1290s, was allegorical from the start.

—Andrew Frisardi

Diane Furtney

Translated from the French of

Arthur Rimbaud

1854 – 1891

Vowels

"Voyelles"

A is black. E, white. I, red. U
is green, O is blue.

One day, O Vowels, I will tell,
not just these details,

but the full, hidden story
of your birth. For now: A is a furry

corset, black, covered in flies that buzz,
glittering, around a vicious stench. A is

also: shadows spreading across
spreading gulfs. E is ingenuousness

of rising vapors; also white tents,
glaciers proud of their icy lances, and upbent,

umbel'd flowers quivering—also the whiteness
of kingship. I is the various

purple-reds: spit-up blood, a mouth
laughing beautifully in rage or bouts

of remorseful drunkenness. U
is the cycles: holy vibrationals moving through

bright-green seas; peaceful fields sprinkled
thickly with animals; peaceful wrinkles

an alchemy imprints
onto dignified, studious faces. But: intense

Trumpet, the supreme
Clarion blasting weird stridencies—extreme

Silences also, intersecting
the Worlds and inter-connecting

the Angels—O is Omega, the sky-blue, a rod,
a straight ray from the eyes of God!

Diane Furtney
Translated from the French of
Armand Sully Prudhomme
1839 – 1907

The Rendezvous
"Le Rendez-vous"

It's very late. But
a persistent, obstinate

astronomer,
at the top of a tower

so remote in the sky
every sound below him has died,

goes on searching between
the golden islands, his head deep-

sunk in the deep night. Infinity
whitens the morning gradually

while he watches: worlds fly about
like sifted grain, crowds

of nebulosities swirl and shine.
Summoning one disheveled sun,

he calls to it, "Come back, exactly here,
in exactly one thousand years."

And that star will return. Not
for a moment of a moment

can it be unfaithful
to inquiry and to something eternal

in the scheduled rendezvous.
Men and women arrive and go, the new

becomes old, but humanity waits
as well for that appointment, looking out

with different individual eyes
but still a steady gaze.

And if, down the centuries,
all humanity dies?

Then Truth itself, hour after hour,
will wait, on the peak that used to hold the tower.

Diane Furtney

Translated from the French of

Gérard de Nerval

1808 – 1855

And It Vanishes

"Épitaphe"

Just now it arrived, immediately at home
as a starling, bright and careless and affectionate just from

newness, though at times glum
and dreamy, head bent, a sad Clitandre[39]. On some

day like any other day, it hears a drum-
noise at the door and—there's death! Not overcome,

not yet, it begs for time
to add a period to its final sonnet. Then: numbed,

moving without moving, at the bottom
of a coffin its body stretches in the tomb

and becomes
colder, then more cold. It had been idle and dumb,

---

39 Clitandre, a stock character especially popular in 17th-century French drama and poetry, is usually a lovesick suitor—young, melancholy, and aristocratic.

and now is more dry than its own inkwell and tomes.
It had wanted knowledge, but at the rim

of existence still knows nothing. In the gloom
of a winter night, when time

takes the last of it and it vanishes like foam,
it leaves asking, "Why did I even come?"

Diane Furtney
Adapted from the French of
François Villon
1431 – c. 1463

What Lasts

Adapted from *"Quatrain,"* in *Poèmes variés* (Miscellaneous Poems),
line 2 of *"Le Lais"* in *Le Testament* and various lines of *Le Testament*

I am François, the cursed, the crass,
Scholar Elegant and Monsieur Smartass,

tough-luck born in Paris,
which everyone knows is

near Pontoise, which is
very near some patch of grass.

And what of it, Bishop, you gorged jackass?
Does your donkey legacy include as

much quintessence of *virtu* as
a hawk or falcon? Or a fish? As

you pray with your grasped
hands, do you own more than my share of the Mass?

Well, I bequeath that to you. As
for the rest, let it pass:

my Averroës commentaries; the gold hasp
I bartered for a sausage and a piece of ass;

and the tavern signs I pilfered: *The Striped Ass*
mounted by *The Duck*. What lasts

is learning: soon a rope will clasp
my fine, learned neck, which will know at last

the exact weight of my ass.

Rachel Hadas
Translated from the Greek of
Euripides
480 BC – 406 BC

Iphigenia in Aulis
   —Lines 334-375

[Menelaus addresses his brother Agamemnon about the mess they're
both in: the proposed sacrifice of Agamemnon's daughter Iphigenia.]

And you have a talent for talking out of both sides of your mouth.
Your friends can never tell which side you're on.
But let me deconstruct the situation.
Stay here. Wait. Don't storm out.
I promise I'll be brief.

          So. When
you were hot to lead the Greeks to Troy
(you didn't want to seem to be on fire
with ambition, but you know you were),
you were available to everyone—
hearty handshakes left and right,
office door never shut,
interviews granted whether people asked for them or not.
You were looking to be visible,
raise your profile, go up in every poll.

Then when you took command—your heart's desire—
your friends found you less friendly than before.
You were no longer so accessible.
But when he's doing well,
exactly then a good man shouldn't change.
On the contrary,
he should help those who've shown him loyalty.
That's when you first disappointed me.

Then, when you got here,
commander of the whole fleet, you became
what? Nothing!
Fate dealt you a stunning blow
the day the gods blocked the favoring wind
needed to send the Greek fleet toward Troy.

So what to do?
The Greek army knew, or thought it knew:
Abandon the expedition.
Forget the whole idea.
Don't waste one more day
waiting on the hopeless dream of Troy.

That spelled the end of your imaginings:
no more ships to command,
no soldiers swarming over Priam's land.
You turned (do you remember?) then to me:
What should I do?

How do I escape this situation,
this hellish corner that I'm painted into?
God forbid, you understand,
that you should lose your power and command,
honor, glory, fame, your burnished name.

Wait. I'm not done.
Then what?
Then when
the prophet Calchas ordered you
to sacrifice your daughter
at Artemis's altar
so that ships could sail across the water
to Troy, you were *relieved*—
(don't say you were not—
finally a way out!)
and promised happily to do just that.
Of your own free will
you sent for the girl.
No one forced you to;
it was only you.
A marriage to Achilles was the lure
you used to bring her here,
to cover up the true
purpose of the altar
where she would meet no bridegroom except slaughter.

And now you've changed your mind a second time.
You wrote a letter

to countermand the order
for Iphigenia to come
to Aulis to her doom.
What could cause such a change?
How strange—
you do not wish to be
your daughter's murderer.
But Agamemnon, this is how things are!
The sky, the sun, the air—
all have heard your word,
your solemn promise to sacrifice her.
You're caught.
There's no way out.

No, wait. Listen.
You're not the only one to fall a victim.
This happens to people all the time.
They bump up against obstacles, back down,
fail. Someone has made a bad decision,
there's some local revolution,
order gives way to dissolution.

As for me,
my heart bleeds, not for you, not for our family,
but for our country. Greece! Poor Greece!
We wanted to accomplish something glorious,
but the barbarians now will laugh at us,
all because of this business with your child.

Whether to sack a city or to lead

an army, it's not courage that you need,

but strategy: wit, brains.

Without intelligence, nothing remains.

For a man bereft

of ingenuity, there's nothing left.

Translator's Note:

In both his tragedies and the plays we'd now classify rather as romances (such as *Helen* or *Iphigenia among the Taurians*), Euripides depicts, with often devastating clarity and realism, men and women in the throes not only of majestic passions like rage or grief but also of humbler but no less pressing dilemmas: What to do? How do I decide? What did that dream mean? Should I tell this secret or not? Did I do the right thing?

    Almost any Euripidean play contains lines which stop the spectator/listener/reader in his or her tracks with their sheer human truth. (I won't quote; they're everywhere.) A master of pathos and irony, a great early voice of protestation against war, a fearless observer of human complexity, at once a deconstructor and an enlivener of the mythical tradition he inherited, Euripides remains one of the world's very greatest dramatists, an endlessly influential artist whose work remains perennially fresh, challenging, and inspiring.

    Euripidean dialogue is relatively clear and simple. His choral lyrics, probably beautiful when set to music and danced, differ markedly from the dialogue in register and diction. These choruses sometimes seem less individual than the dialogue and more interchangeable from one play to the next. But they have a pathos and a formal complexity that always complement (sometimes to ironic effect) the barer, more colloquial texture of the spoken dialogue.

—Rachel Hadas

Jay Hopler
Translated from the German of
Georg Trakl
1887 – 1914

The Rats

"Die Ratten"

Autumn moonlight, the courtyard is white with it.
Fantastic shadows fall from the eaves.
A silence lives in the empty windows;
Then the rats up from the sewer come

Quietly and flit, whistling, here and there,
And the grizzly smell of shit whiffs
Out after them, quivering through the light
Of that spooky moon.

And they bicker, greedy, ravenous,
And rush into the house and barns full of corn
And fruits. The winds whine, icy,
In the darkness.

Jay Hopler
Translated from the German of
Georg Trakl
1887 – 1914

Evening Thunderstorm

"Der Gewitterabend"

                          O the red evening hours!
A glimmering falters past the open window.
Grape leaves loop woozily through the blue gloom,
Worried ghosts nestling inside them.

Dust dances in the stinking gutters.
The wind rattles the windowpanes.
A stampede of thunderbolts drives
Before it the dazzling clouds.

With a crash, the glassy pond shatters.
A colony of seagulls clamors by the window frames.
A fiery dragon springs from the hills
And explodes into flames in the pines.

In the hospital, the suffering shriek.
The night's bluish plumage buzzes.
The rain, glittering, thunders down
Upon the roofs.

Jay Hopler
Translated from the German of
Georg Trakl
1887 – 1914

Amen

"Amen"

A ghost floats through the rotten parlor;
    Shadows on the yellow wallpapers; in dark mirrors arch
    Our hands' ivory sadness.
Brown pearls stream through the dead fingers.
    In the stillness,
    The blue eyes of an angel open up like poppies.
The evening is also blue;
    Our hour of death, Azrael's shadow,
    A brown garden darkens.

Teresa Iverson

Translated from the German of

Nelly Sachs

1891 – 1970

Five Poems

I.

"Wenn ich nur wüßte"

If only I knew,
what your last look rested on.
Was it a stone that had already drunk
many last looks, until they fell in blindness
on the blind?

Or was it dirt,
earth enough to fill a shoe,
and already turned black
from so many good-byes
and from causing so much death?

Or was it your last road,
that brought you the farewell from all roads
you had walked on?

A puddle, a piece of mirroring metal,
the belt buckle of your enemy, perhaps,
or any other small fortune-teller
of heaven?

Or did this Earth, that doesn't allow
anyone to depart from here unloved,
send a bird-sign through the air,
reminding your soul so that it flinched
in its body burned with anguish?

II.
"Chor der Waisen"

Chorus of Orphans

We orphans
We lament the world:
Our branch was cut down
And thrown into the fire—
Out of our protectors, they made firewood—
We orphans lie on the fields of Loneliness.
We orphans
We lament the world:
In the night our parents play hide-and-seek with us—
Behind the black folds of Night
Their faces study us,
Their mouths are saying something:
We were dry wood in a woodcarver's hand—
But our eyes have become angel-eyes
And look at you,
They see through the black
Folds of Night—
We orphans
We lament the world:
Our toys have become stones,
Stones have faces, Father- and Mother-faces
They don't wilt like flowers, they don't bite like animals—
And they don't burn like dry wood, when one throws it in the oven—

We orphans we lament the world:
World why have you taken our tender Mothers
And our Fathers, who said: My child, you resemble me!
We orphans, who no longer resemble anyone in the world!
O World,
It's you we accuse!

III.

    "Engel der Bittenden"

Angel of suppliants,
now, where the fire like a rending sunset
scorched all habitation to night—
walls and utensils, the hearth and the cradle,
all fallen parcels of longing—
longing, that flies in the blue sail of air!

Angel of suppliants,
on Death's white floor, that supports nothing any more,
grows the forest planted in despair.
Forest of arms with branches of hands,
nails dug into the castle of Night, into the stars' mantel.
Or else plowing Death, him, the one who preserves life.

Angel of suppliants,
in the forest that doesn't rustle
where shadows are painters of the dead
and transparent tears of lovers
the seed-corn.
Mesmerized by the moon, the mothers
tear out their roots as if seized by the storm,
and creaking, the old men's dead wood decays.
But the children are still playing in the sand,
practicing, forming something new out of the Night
since they are still warm from transformation.

Angel of suppliants,
bless the sand,
let it understand the language of longing,
from this something new wants to grow from a child's hand,
always something new!

IV.
> *"Wenn der Tag leer wird"*

When the day empties itself
in the twilight,
when the imageless time begins,
the lonely voices join together—
the animals are nothing other than the hunting
or hunted—
the flowers no more than fragrance—
when everything becomes nameless as in the beginning—
you go under the catacombs of Time,
which open for those that are near the end—
there where the heart buds grow—
into the dark inwardliness
you sink downward—
already past death
which is only a windy passageway—
and freezing from going out
you open your eyes
where a new star
has already left its reflection—

V.
    "Der Schlafwandler"

The sleepwalker
circling on his star
in the white feather of morning
wakes up—
the spot of blood on it calls it to mind—
lets the moon fall startled—
the snowberry shatters
on Night's black agate
dirtied with dreams—

No pure white on Earth—

Julie Kane, *with* **the author** *and* **Rima Krasauskytė**
Translated from the Lithuanian of
Tautvyda Marcinkevičiūtė
b. 1954

The Hardest Work

"Sunkiausias darbas"

And he assigned some work:
Until the sun came up
To scrub, rinse, and wring
Through a hole in the ice,
To dry in the sun,
To press with a steam iron
The funeral garments.

And he assigned some work:
Until the sun came up
From pink damask roses
And the whitest of lilies,
From myrtles and herbs,
To weave a funeral wreath,
To engrave an inscription
They'd read in the valley of Joseph.

And he assigned some work:
Until the sun came up
To soothe the frightened brothers
And sisters of the deceased,
To stroke their little heads and tender hands,
To explain the meaning of death to them.

And he assigned some work:
Until the sun came up
To catch the tears spurting at difficult moments,
To dry them with kisses.

And he assigned some work:
Until the sun came up
To glue his son's body parts back together,
To dig small canals so the blood could run through them,
To open the sticky lashes,
To make the cold lips speak,
And to blow incomprehensible life back through them.

Julie Kane

Translated from the French of

Victor Hugo

1802 – 1885

She Picked Up the Habit

"Elle avait pris ce pli"

She picked up the habit, when she was a toddler,
Of coming in my room first thing in the morning,
Welcome as a sunbeam as I sat there waiting.
The first thing she'd say would be, "Good morning, Daddy."
Then she would grab my pen, open books, clamber up
On my bed, scatter all my papers, and giggle;
Then suddenly leave like a migratory bird.
Refreshed, I'd resume the work she'd interrupted;
And every so often, while I was revising
One of my manuscripts, I'd stumble across
Some crazy arabesque scribbled in the margins,
Or sometimes a blank page crumpled between her hands
On which, don't ask me how, my best verses took shape.
She loved God, stars, meadows—meadows full of flowers;
She was a spirit inside a female body;
To look at her, you'd see the brightness of her soul;
And I was the lucky one she chose to seek out.
Now, I think back to those sparkling winter evenings
Spent studying language, history, and grammar,

My four children balanced on my knees, their mother
Chatting with a neighbor at the fireside, close by.
I'd return to that life, be content with little—
But to say that she's dead: God have mercy on me!
I could never be happy, sensing she felt sad;
I would be depressed at the most elegant ball
If, leaving, I had seen some shadow in her eyes.

Translator's Note:

"She Picked Up the Habit" mourns the death of Hugo's daughter Léopoldine, who was only 19 when she drowned in a boating accident.

—*Julie Kane*

X.J. Kennedy
Translated from the French of
Arthur Rimbaud
1854 – 1891

Sensation

Blue summer nights, along far paths I'll go,
Needled by wheat stalks, stubbled grass—ah, how
I'll dream, feeling the cool with each bare toe,
Letting the breeze caress my naked brow.

An infinite passion rising in my soul.
I'll say no word and let no thought abide,
But far through Nature take my gypsy stroll,
Happy as with a woman by my side.

X.J. Kennedy
Translated from the French of
Arthur Rimbaud
1854 – 1891

Evil

When the red spittle of machine gun fire
Whistles all day through infinite blue sky,
When scarlet and green battalions collapse before
A heartless King who jeers them as they die,

When an enormous folly makes a pyre
Of a hundred thousand smoking corpses, when
In summer, in the grass—pathetic dead!—
Nature! with joy you sanctify those men!—

There is a God who laughs at chalices
Of gold; at incense, damask altar cloths,
Who falls asleep by loud hosannas lulled,

But wakes whenever flocks of mourning mothers
In their black bonnets, weeping, wailing griefs,
Bring Him small coins knotted in handkerchiefs.

X.J. Kennedy
Translated from the French of
Arthur Rimbaud
1854 – 1891

My sad heart snivels on the poop

    Deck, slathered with tobacco juice,
    Pelted with squirts of spat-out soup.
    My sad heart snivels on the poop
    Deck at the torrent of the crew's
    Derisive laughter and abuse.
    My sad heart snivels on the poop
    Deck, slathered with tobacco juice.

    Stiff-phallused as an infantry,
    Their jeers have left my heart depraved,
    The vessel's helm with forms engraved
    Stiff-phallused as an infantry.
    Abracadabra-chanting waves,
    Come wash my heart and set it free!
    Stiff-phallused as an infantry,
    Their jeers have left my heart depraved.

When all their vile quid-chawing halts,
What shall we do, my ravished heart?
They'll belch and hiccup, soused old salts,
When all their vile quid-chawing halts.
My stomach will turn somersaults.
I'll feel defiled when they depart,
When all their vile quid-chawing halts—
What shall we do, my ravished heart?

Translator's Note:

The preceding three poems of Arthur Rimbaud are some of the great French poet's earliest (1870 – 71). Among them, *"Le Coeur volé"* [Ravished Heart], has least often been translated. Its problems for a translator include its ninth line: *"Ithyphalliques et pioupiesques."*

—*X.J. Kennedy*

Kent Leatham

Translated from the Scots of

Gavin Douglas

1474 – 1522

from **Book 7 of** *Eneados*

(in which the Latins prepare for war against the Trojans)

Long unstirred, becalmed, Italy
Instantly erupts in martial fury:
Foot soldiers flood the fertile fields
As lords on horseback strut behind their shields,
Trampling the earth to a frenzy of dust.
Each man seeks the weapon he loves most:
Some polish spearheads till the steel gleams;
Some burnish armor, massaging the seams
With grease and lard; some slowly hone
The blades of axes on sleek whetstones.
All are proud to let their pennons fly,
And all rejoice at the trumpet's cry.

Five of the greatest and chiefest of cities
Bring to blazing life their weaponries:
They fashion forges whose steel anvils ring:
Rich Atina, and haughty Tiburine,
Ardea the jewel, and Crustumerium,
And Antemnae graced by tower and column

And ringed all round with war-proof walls:
In each city's forge the hammer stroke falls,
As smiths well-skilled in metal and flame
Summon forth breastplate, barding, and helm,
Bend willow branches to brace their targes,
Stretch leather on bucklers to shield their charges,
Knit hauberks together, link by steel link,
Buff poleyns, schynbalds, and faulds for the flank,
Enameling each piece with the star-shine of silver.
Hungry for iron and steel, they pilfer
Plows for coulters, soams, and shares;
Likewise, all scythes and harvesting shears
Are brought, dismantled, and recast:
The tools of peace are now things of the past,
Wholly transformed into weapons for knights
To safeguard their country and maintain their rights.

Once they assemble their weapons and gear,
The draft-trumpet blasts the challenge of war.
The command is passed from rank to rank:
"The battle draws nigh; we stand on the brink."
The foot soldier tugs his helmet down
To muffle his fear in the din of the throng.
The charioteer drives his steeds to the yoke;
They stamp and snort and sweat and smoke.
The captain swaggers behind his great shield,
Wrapped in his hauberk of steel laced with gold.
His corslet, breastplate, and terrible sword
Have cut from their tongues the plow's peaceful word.

Kent Leatham

Translated from the Scots of

William Fowler

1560 – 1612

Sonnet: In Orkney

"Sonet. In Orknay"

Upon the utmost corners of the world,
and on the borders of this planet round,
where by fate and fortune I've been hurled,
I deplore my griefs upon this ground:

seeing roaring seas from rocks rebound
by ebbs and streams of stubborn surging tides,
and Phoebus' chariot in their waves lying drowned,
who equally now the night and day divides,

I call to mind the storms my thoughts abide,
which ever wax and never deign to wane,
for in day's joy my nights of evil hide,
and in their vales suppress my poor design:

this I see, wherever I may range—
I change but seas; my love I cannot change.

Kent Leatham
Translated from the Scots of
William Dunbar
1460 – 1520

The Two Old Nags

"The Twa Cummeris"

Early one Ash Wednesday dawn,
Two gossips sat, guzzling wine.
Leaning a hand on her corpulent knee,
Groaning and swigging, the first complained,
"This long Lent is starving me."

On a couch beside the fire she sat,
And God knows she was grossly fat,
But feigned such feeble frailty,
And sighed, "Let this be proof of that:
Christ, this Lent is starving me."

"My dear, sweet hag," coughed the other,
"You got that tightness from your mother,
Who shunned wine in all variety
But Malmsey, in which she would get smothered;
Oh, this long Lent is starving me."

"Crone, be glad now and tomorrow,
Though you're forced to beg and borrow;
You should refrain from misery,
And let your husband suffer the sorrow;
Lord, this long Lent is starving me."

"Your counsel, witch, is good," said the first,
"To piss him off, I'll do my worst;
In bed, the man's not worth a flea.
Fill my glass, for I am cursed:
This long Lent is starving me."

They tippled from a half-pint cup,
And drank two quarts, sip by sup;
Their thirst was such as no man knew,
Because they drank from hungry hope—
Lent would never starve those two!

R.C. Neighbors
Translated from the German of
Bertolt Brecht
1898 – 1956

Of the Drowned Girl

"Vom ertrunkenen Mädchen"

1.
When she had drowned and floated down,
from the streams into the larger rivers,
the opal of heaven shone wonderfully,
as if it had to soothe the corpse.

2.
Seaweed and algae held to her,
so she gradually became heavier.
Cold fish swam against her leg—
the plants and animals, a burden on her last journey.

3.
And the evening sky became as dark as smoke
and at night held the light in balance with the stars.
But soon the light grew bright, so there
would still be morning and evening for her.

4.
When her pale flesh had rotted in the water,
it happened that God slowly, so slowly, forgot her—
first her face, then the hands and finally her hair.
She became carrion in the rivers full of carrion.

Kate Light *and* Michael Palma

Translated from the Italian of

Antonio Malatesti

1610 – c. 1672

Riddles

—Published in *La Sfinge* (1640)

1.

The World is made from nothing, nothing I am,
    And all returns to this nothing eventually;
    Men tremble at the mention of my name,
    But cannot rest until they come to me.
I am called blessing, curse, catastrophe
    By those who are mad, or sad, or without blame;
    The ones who know me never can get free,
    And those who don't, can share me all the same.
Some call me in their agonized condition,
    But then prefer all other company,
    Though for grave illness I am the physician.
I work my will, my will's allowed to be;
    So just and of such liberal disposition,
    I'll give myself to the one who fashioned me.[40]

---

40   Answer: See "Riddle Notes" on page 175.

2.

Whoever wants to see what slips away
> but cannot, let him stand in front of me.
> If he has wits about him, eyes to see,
> he'll surely recognize what I display.

Since I have no religion and no faith,
> it's by the power of silver that I act.
> I show the body as it is in fact,
> undressed, unless I'm clothed by human breath.

Though ugly people greet me angrily
> and beauties smile, no matter what you do
> I'll always clearly tell the truth to you.

Little and large are less and more to me;
> but if I weren't so fragile, I would be
> worth more than the whole nation of Peru.[41]

---

[41] Answer: See "Riddle Notes" on page 175.

Michael Palma
Translated from the Italian of
Giovanni Raboni
1932 – 2004

"*Sono quello che eravate...*"

I'm what you were, it won't be long before
I'm what you are, I murmur to anyone
who spies me walking by from a bed upon
the ward of the Niguarda pavilion or

the hall of the old polyclinic on
the Via Sforza, you credit me with more
than I deserve, soon I will lose my war
with myopia, now I have only one

kidney, and oh the heart, the heart. . . . But no,
dear souls, I beg your pardon, I cannot
play Death's anointed here, nobody ought

to teach the art of dying to those who
are dying so much already, whose hopes are few,
only another spring, another snow.

Michael Palma
Translated from the Italian of
Giovanni Raboni
1932 – 2004

"Fra L'anschluss e la notte dei cristalli..."

Between the Anschluss and the Kristallnacht,
between Munich and Danzig I could place
precisely in that period those few days
of *ecuméne,* when the dances lacked

phantoms, days when all my people who
are never absent were truly present, there
as vassals of the sunlight and the air
in the intervals of the dream of death. . . . Are you

really certain of it, though? and then that drive
past city gates and tollhouse, far from home,
led by the first to disappear, his own

Charon, nothing then but skin and bone
at the wheel of the last, the shiniest, most chrome-
decorated convertible of his whole life?

Michael Palma
Translated from the Italian of
Giovanni Raboni
1932 – 2004

"La casa di campagna..."

The house out in the country where I'd stay
awake reading Forster or George Eliot till
the hour of ashes and even then the still
of the hedges invigorating me to play

cards with those not yet gone away, I find
the image of those times the single thing
that brings me pleasure when I'm hovering
on the landslide of sleep. But then the mind,

awakening a little later, buoyed
by childish hunger for the light of day
to seize the horrid sweetness of the now

intrepidly, forgets it: and that's how
one foot trips over the other, that's the way
we undo the invisible mending of the void.

Michael Palma
Translated from the Italian of
Fosildo Mirtunzio *(Pseudonym)*
1610 – c. 1672

Riddles

—published in *Veglie autunnali* (1796)

1.

A harbinger of peace and tranquility
    When loud and violent storms have dissipated,
    Above the highest pinnacles I'll be,
    Painted in varied colors and concentrated.
    Unfathomable in immensity,
    Along my secret ways I'll soon have faded.
    A Star tints me, and when it goes I go,
    And I unveil myself in saying so.[42]

---

[42] Answer: See "Riddle Notes" on page 175.

2.

I am your faithful servant, night and day,
    A field beside you none can separate;
    Make just the slightest move, and straightaway
    Your every act I darkly imitate;
    I make my home with you, with you I stay,
    Nor can I ever change my fine estate,
    For I escort you daily in the light,
    And torches sometimes steer me in the night.[43]

---

43   Answer: See "Riddle Notes" on page 175.

ESSAY

Michael Palma
"Against the Daily Grind"

Like most people who are seriously involved with poetry, I made my earliest discoveries and formed my first enthusiasms by way of anthologies. Happening on Roy J. Cook's *101 Famous Poems* in my tiny local public library (two rooms on the basement floor of the elementary school), I developed an early taste for patriotic ditties and sentimental ballads—although I fail, no doubt self-servingly, to recall ever enjoying the rhymester of whom Oscar Williams observed that "Edgar Guest/ Is never at his best." My taste took a large leap forward when I found Louis Untermeyer's *Treasury of Great Poems, English and American*. Some have complained that its selections are unimaginative, its textual discussions superficial, its biographical sketches romanticized; there is some truth in all these observations, yet it was just the right book at just the right moment, a doorway into an endlessly unfolding room that I have never found my way out of. Untermeyer is undervalued nowadays, when he is remembered at all, owing in part to the snotty epigram by E. E. Cummings that begins "mr u will not be missed"; Cummings's charge that Untermeyer used his anthologies for self-promotion is, in fact, much more applicable to the aforementioned Oscar Williams: reviewing one of Williams's anthologies, Randall Jarrell wrote: "There are nine of his poems—and five of Hardy's. It takes a lot of courage to like your own poetry almost twice as well as Hardy's."

But my adolescent progress may have differed from the usual pattern in one significant respect: at the same time that I was developing a serious interest in poetry, I was also developing a serious interest in poetry in translation. This state of affairs was indirectly brought about by, of all things, the movies. In the summer of 1962, a few months before I turned seventeen, I began working as an usher at the local movie theater. In the middle of the next block was a store where I would go for coffee on my breaks and for a sandwich on my dinner hour. It was a big-tent kind of place, a combination lunch counter, stationery, toy store, and bookshop. One of the owners was a man of some sophistication and good taste, because the books were not the mass-market best sellers of Mickey Spillane, Grace Metalious, or even Erskine Caldwell; they were serious works of literature and academic studies, including an extensive run of Modern Library hardcovers, both regular editions and Giants, as well as a generous sampling from the then nascent field of trade paperbacks. Almost immediately I became a regular buyer, and virtually every evening I walked out with a book or two along with—or, when necessary, instead of—my dinner.

Among the books I bought there were many that I fondly recall and some that are still on my shelves, among them the anthologies edited by Angel Flores for the Doubleday Anchor series. Reading the versions of Christian Morgenstern in his *Anthology of German Poetry from Hölderlin to Rilke,* I saw that only by attempting to duplicate his rhythms and sound effects could the poems be made to work in English, as in the one (in R. F. C. Hull's translation) about the pike and his wife who were converted by Saint Anthony to a vegetarian diet: "But cake, grass, porridge, they would find/ Flowed out disastrously behind." In the *Anthology of French Poetry from Nerval to Válery,* I was overwhelmed by Apollinaire, especially by the darts and swoops of imagination in "Zone" as translated by Dudley Fitts. Then, when I discovered another translation of this poem, done by the editor himself in Selden Rodman's *100 Modern Poems,* I read the two side by side, looking for similarities and taking note of differences, and, thus, by stumbling into my first comparative exercise, I had my first glimmers of awareness of both the freedoms and the constraints of poetic translation.

The Rodman anthology was pivotal. I read through it and its companion volume, *100 American Poems,* in the little gold Signet paperbacks, and I found myself going back much more frequently to the *Modern.* Some of its poems were opaque and others were somewhat silly (and fifty years later some of them still are), but all in all the collection had a zest and variety and unexpectedness that made many of the pieces in the American anthology seem stiff and stale by comparison; I had already come a long way from *101 Famous Poems.* And from *100 Modern Poems* I took away an unconscious but very important awareness that would be a basis for much of the work that I would subsequently do. The book was divided into four sections: the first (about a third of the volume) was made up of poems translated from a number of European languages; the rest of the collection was poetry written in English. Despite the segregation, all the poems coexisted on an equal footing. So, from my very beginnings as a serious reader of poetry, I saw translations not as poor relations or inadequate substitutes, but as works of art just as real and valid as any others.

One of the poems in that first section of Rodman's anthology was Vladimir Mayakovsky's "At the Top of My Voice," in Herbert Marshall's translation. My eye slid down page after page of it, carried along by the poem's vigor and swagger and shamelessly in-your-face attitude: "For you,/ who're so healthy and nimble,/ a poet/ licked up/ consumptive spittle/

with the crude rough tongue of placards." I'd never heard of anyone who thought such things, let alone wrote them down for all the world to see. I wanted to read more of this Mayakovsky, and I had my chance, because the store down the street from the movie theater had a copy of his *The Bedbug and Selected Poetry,* the original paperback edition with the cover photograph of the poet in his cap looking less self-conscious and more vulnerable than usual. I bought it and fell upon it hungrily. I was fascinated by the rapid pace of the short step-down lines of most of the poems, by the utter freedom with which the poet wrote, by the oddity of a Soviet poet writing something called "Brooklyn Bridge" and addressing Calvin Coolidge in the very first line. But the poem that intrigued me the most was the last one in the book. It was totally different from everything that had come before. It was very short, only twelve lines. It was in blank verse. And, in strong contrast to the boisterous, bumptious, and frequently crude strut of the author's customary style, it had a hushed and somber feel to it. Titled after its opening phrase, it was called "Past One O'Clock...":

> Past one o'clock. You must have gone to bed.
> The Milky Way streams silver through the night.
> I'm in no hurry; with lightning telegrams
> I have no cause to wake or trouble you.
> And, as they say, the incident is closed.
> Love's boat has smashed against the daily grind.
> Now you and I are quits. Why bother then
> To balance mutual sorrows, pains, and hurts.
> Behold what quiet settles on the world.
> Night wraps the sky in tribute from the stars.
> In hours like these, one rises to address
> The ages, history, and all creation.

According to the notes, this poem was by way of a suicide note, written shortly before Mayakovsky's death, at thirty-six, by gunshot on April 14, 1930. Parts of it existed in several drafts and versions—in one of them the beginning of the seventh line read "Now life and I are quits"—and it was presumably addressed to his long-time married lover, Lili Brik. It was widely assumed that his breakup with her, or possibly another woman, had driven him to kill himself. (Starting at almost the moment of Mayakovsky's death and continuing down to the present, there has been constant controversy over whether this was in fact his motivation. It has also been claimed that he was disillusioned over Stalin's betrayal of the Revolution. And there are those who wonder whether he actually committed suicide at all.)

Interesting as these details were, I was much more taken by the text itself. I read it again and again, as if it were a mechanism that I could take apart and put back together to understand how it worked. The first line established the setting and situation with striking economy (or at least it created a setting in my mind: I've always had an image of the speaker alone in his quiet room, although there's nothing in the text to base it on: for all I know, he could be standing outside looking up at the sky). The poem's indirectness about the situation was one of the things that held me; unlike many of the modern poems I had read, it contained no deliberate obscurantism or showy illogical phrasing, but it was just coy enough about the relationship at its heart to keep me coming back to it. The quiet tone maintained throughout the poem added powerfully to its air of resignation and transcendence of life's petty concerns. The last two lines especially haunted me. Without trying to, I committed them to memory, and they would pop into my head at odd times, for no reason at all that I could trace, just as they continue to do to this day. More than anything else, they impressed me with the way that they moved and enlarged the poem from its mundane opening to a sublime conclusion in just a few lines—a progression I would later find even more strikingly charted in Philip Larkin's "High Windows."

Except for some awkwardness in the third and fourth lines, I found—and still find—the translation to be finely wrought and totally effective. Even in my poetic innocence and inexperience, I sensed that the translator had worked carefully and hard to achieve these effects. The translators of *The Bedbug and Selected Poetry* were Max Hayward and George Reavey. Hayward had translated the title play and one of the poems, while the rest of the poetry, including "Past One O'Clock . . . ," had been done by Reavey. Remembered principally, if at all, for his many translations from Russian literature, Reavey had what was, by any measurement, an unusual career. He was a close friend of Samuel Beckett's and acted at various times as Beckett's literary agent and even his publisher; his Europa Press brought out Beckett's *Echo's Bones* in 1935, and also published volumes by Denis Devlin and Paul Eluard (in translations by Reavey, Beckett, and others) and several collections of Reavey's own poetry. Fallen into neglect and poverty in New York in the 1950s, he translated and edited some of the manuscript material of a young and unknown Jerzy Kosinski, and later claimed to have written *The Painted Bird*. After Reavey's death, Beckett wrote: "Adieu George, to whom I owed so much, with whom shared so much, for whom cared so much."

At both the beginning and the end of his career, Reavey published his poetry in limited editions with small and sometimes tiny presses, but in between he enjoyed a bit of currency with *The Colours of Memory,* issued by Grove Press in 1955 during its brief pre-Barney Rosset incarnation, when it was more interested in Henry James than Henry Miller; poetry lovers of a certain age will no doubt remember the dull blue-gray cover of the paperback edition. There is a fair amount of variety in both style and subject in its sixty pages, but insofar as Reavey can be said to have an identifiable manner, the following stanza is as representative as any: "Word, smash the four walls of my cage,/ The four imprisoning reasons,/ The four strong empires of my age,/ And all four-footed seasons." This sounds almost nothing like Reavey's translation of Mayakovsky, and that, I think, is greatly to his credit.

"Past One O'Clock . . ." was one of my earliest lessons in the translator's invisibility—and, all too often, anonymity. (This was a lesson that I learned, if anything, too well: for a long time, I casually assumed that the poem had been translated by Hayward. It chills me to recall that Reavey's own poetry is now completely forgotten, but it ruefully consoles me to think that without his translations he would be as well.) Thanks to the translator's notes, it taught several other lessons about the dilemmas and difficulties of translation. He pointed out that "[i]n the original, the Milky Way is compared to the Oka River, an effluent of the Volga"; every translator has no doubt wrestled with the issue of how to handle obscure local references. Even more depressingly, Reavey's notes confessed that the phrase "the incident is closed" contained an untranslatable pun.

But the chief lesson that I learned from this little poem is one that has been a bedrock of my own intentions, which is that to be truly successful a translation must also be a successful work of art in English. This lesson would be brought home to me over and over again, as when, for instance, my first encounters with *Faust* and *Madame Bovary* left me wondering what all the fuss was about, until I turned to other, better translations. "Past One O'Clock . . ." is reprinted in Michael Almereyda's 2008 volume *Night Wraps the Sky: Writings by and about Mayakovsky*. In fact, Almereyda's title is taken from one of its lines: "Night wraps the sky in tribute from the stars." Whenever I come across another version of Mayakovsky, I look immediately to see what has been done with this poem, and a quick look at some other renderings of that line will suggest something of the extent of Reavey's accomplishment:

> Night tributes the sky/ with silver constellations.
>
> Night has covered the sky with a starlit tribute.
>
> The sky/ is paying a starry tribute/ to the night.
>
> The starry night is grandiose and spacious.

In 2000 Carmela Ciuraru published *First Loves: Poets Introduce the Essential Poems that Captivated & Inspired Them,* in which we learn, among other things, that Robert Creeley was captivated by "The Highwayman" and A.R. Ammons was inspired by "In Flanders Fields." I'm sure that many other poets have thought, as I have, about what their own choices would be. I suppose there's a certain aptness to the fact that my choice is a translation. I have no idea how accurately "Past One O'Clock" reflects what Vladimir Mayakovsky actually wrote, and I doubt that I ever will. But it has stayed in my head for fifty years, and it gave me an enthusiasm for Mayakovsky that I will never lose. In Maureen McLane's *My Poets* (2012), the section entitled "My Translated: An Abecedary" is made up entirely of such sentences as "My Baudelaire is Louise Varèse, as is my Rimbaud" and "My Rilke is Stephen Mitchell, irrevocably." Following her lead, I can state unequivocally that my Mayakovsky is George Reavey, and always will be.

Deborah Ann Percy and **Arnold Johnston,** with **Dona Roşu**
Translated from the Romanian of
Zaharia Stancu
1902 – 1974

The Days, The Days
"Zilele, Zilele"

I don't know how my days were,
But to the very last, they burned, they burned.
Their ash lay on my palm.
The wind came and blew it away
Over flowering gardens, blew it away.

I don't know how my nights were,
But to the very last, they melted
Like the winter snows, they melted.
The earth opened his mouth, his mouth,
And to the very last, he swallowed them.

I don't know how my love was,
Was she sweet or was she sour?
She may have lasted a life entire, or maybe just one night.
The villain Time brought her on his wings.
The villain Time came and took her back.

I don't know how my death will be,
But she won't be gentle.
Too much I've longed for her, too much I've hated her,
Too much I've called for her; now it's too late to hope she'll go away.
Too much I've called for her.

Deborah Ann Percy and ***Arnold Johnston***, with ***Dona Roşu***
Translated from the Romanian of
Zaharia Stancu
1902 – 1974

The Fourth Horse
"Al Patrulea Cal"

When I was a lad I rode
A white horse, like St. George.
The horse had no wings, and I no arrow,
But just like St. George I slew green dragons,
A dragon-slayer I, just like St. George.

When my moustache appeared, I was riding through the world,
A gray horse I was riding.
The horse had no wings, nor had I,
But both of us could leap over mountains,
Over rivers. . . . Young! How young we were! . . .

Later on I rode a dark bay horse.
Oh, how his hooves struck fire!
Come with me, fair maid, I said,
To each fair maid I met.
My horse has a saddle of gold.

Now I wait at by the roadside, wait by the roadside,
For the fourth horse to appear.
How will the fourth horse look?
The fourth horse will have wings.
The fourth horse will be black,
Black . . . black as tar.

Deborah Ann Percy and *Arnold Johnston,* with *Dona Roşu*

Translated from the Romanian of

Zaharia Stancu

1902 – 1974

Man at Sunset

"Om în Amurg"

Now I'm a man at sunset,
Run back among your mountains, doe,
I wish no more to kiss your lips
A second, a third time, no more
Now I'm a man at sunset
Be gone from me, you banker sly
I've no more interest in your gold
Gold has no weight in the sky

Each day brings its sunset
Each day its dawn also
In fall the vine is full of grapes
In springtime only flowers grow

Now I'm a man at sunset
The midday hour was sweet, was sweet
And in its nest of snowflakes
The moon soon fell asleep

Translators' Note:

These translations of poems by Stancu represent a joint effort by three writers: Deborah Ann Percy, my wife and frequent collaborator; Dona Roşu, the fine Romanian poet and non-fiction writer; and me, Arnold Johnston. Over ten years ago the playwright Hristache Popescu asked Dona to translate two of his one-act plays—*Night of the Passions* (Noaptea Patimilor) and *Sons of Cain* (Fii Lui Cain)—from Romanian into English. Dona then approached Debby and me because of our extensive playwriting experience and because she knew about my translations of songs by Jacques Brel. Dona wanted to make sure that, when rendered in English, the Popescu plays conformed to professional dramatic format; she also expressed uncertainty that her own command of English would ensure properly idiomatic dialogue. Over a period of months the three of us produced the finished translations, which were eventually published together in Bucharest by Editura HP (1999). Since then we have worked on a number of other projects, including plays, a memoir by Dona's late husband, Lucian Roşu, and Dona's own wonderful poetry.

Our method of translation has remained essentially the same. All three of us sit around a table while Dona reads from the piece to be translated. She renders the Romanian into literal English, while Debby (or I) writes a more idiomatic version on a legal pad, discussing our choices wherever necessary. Once we've completed each day's transcription, I type up the results, making some improvements as I do, then share the draft with Dona and Debby for further discussion. Our translations of Stancu's poems, a project for which Dona had expressed great enthusiasm, followed this method, facilitated by her native fluency in Romanian, her poetic talent, a good dictionary, and a good thesaurus. Debby's and my qualifications were our being native speakers and writers—of poetry, lyrics, fiction, drama, and nonfiction—in English, the language into which we were translating the poems—as well as our being experienced translators.

Catching the letter and the spirit of someone's work demands the ability to be your own thesaurus for units of thought larger than individual words, to find the right idiomatic expression among a range of choices, and to express a thought in a number of ways, with appropriate attention to emotional nuance and wit. The vital requirement for any writer is having the linguistic resources to provide yourself with choices, rather than being stuck with your first attempt, whether the task at hand is translation or original composition in your native tongue

Of Stancu's fiction, critic Andre Kedros said in *Les Nouvelles litteraires:* "By his storyteller's gift and by the gentle love he shows even to his most debased fellow men, Zaharia Stancu is . . . Gorky's worthiest heir in contemporary literature . . . "; and the *Washington Post* called Stancu "a storyteller in the tradition of Sholokhov." Stancu's poetry, as may be seen in these translations, obviously shares the qualities of his prose, especially in evoking the people and landscape of his native country and in achieving a diction that, like Thomas Hardy's, embodies a vision both romantic and bleakly deterministic, at once sophisticated and evocative of a folktale's simplicity.

Poetry is often cited as the most difficult writing to capture in another language, because even in its original form a poem attempts to reach beyond the very limits of language. The considerable linguistic challenge posed by poetic translation often means that translators refrain from attempting to deal with the further complications of form, metrics, sound devices, and the like. My experience in translating songs, especially in singable versions, has encouraged me to believe that one needn't back away from most of these challenges. In any case, one of my major contributions to this group of Stancu's poems was in creating the rhymed version of "Man at Sunset."

Otherwise, my efforts, and those of my admirable collaborators have been guided by our commitment to rendering Stancu's poems in English that comes as close as possible to the original Romanian in meaning, spirit, and form, and that introduces an aspect of this distinguished writer's work to a world that knows him chiefly as a novelist.

—Arnold Johnston

―――――――――――――
Translator's Preface:

Rilke wrote over four hundred poems in French. Many of these poems incorporate ideas, tropes, and idioms that abound in his German poetry, such as the iconic symbol of the rose. The prose poems in French are an interesting occurrence; they demonstrate his willingness to play with form, even in another language. The inspiration for "Circus Performers" comes from a Picasso painting, "La Famille de saltimbanques," which captures a group of itinerant entertainers with disaffected and melancholy expressions. Likewise, a line from "Cemetery" describing a rose as "no one's sleep under so many eyelids" echoes Rilke's self-chosen epitaph: *"Rose, oh reiner Widerspruch, Lust/ Niemandes Schlaf zu sein/ unter soviel/ Lidern"* [Rose, oh pure contradiction, joy/ no one's sleep/ under so many eyelids].

—Maria Picone

Maria Picone

Translated from the French of

Rainer Maria Rilke

1875 – 1926

Circus Performers

"Saltimbanques"

1

Our path isn't wider than yours; we often fall from the top and are broken, but our inattention doesn't force us to remount the rope. The slightest mistake could kill you. We, with our thousand errors, amuse the onlooker Death, who has the best seat in the circus of our misfortunes.

2

Let's play like them: never falling without dying. What a crowd around our drop! But a child, a little way off, stares at the empty rope against the backdrop of the undisturbed night.

3

The rope was so high that it spread itself out above the spotlights. In a while it would be among us wearing its too-pink leotard. Above, however, its rosy otherness would explain to the vast night the absurdity of its pure, unstable danger.

4

If such perfection dwelled in the soul, what saints you would make! The soul *is* that capable, but the saints touch it only by accident, in the uncommon opportunities of an imperceptible clumsiness.

Maria Picone
Translated from the French of
Rainer Maria Rilke
1875 – 1926

For Monique

—a small meditation on my gratitude

Teatime

Drinking from this teacup on which, in an unknown language, there are (perhaps) inscriptions of blessing and good luck, I hold it in my hand, which also has mysterious lines I cannot explain. Are these two scripts in agreement? and since they are alone together and eternally hidden under the dome of my gaze, can they converse in their way and become friends, these two antiquated texts brought closer by the gesture of drinking?

Rustic Chapel

How calm the house is: listen! But inside the white chapel, from where does that surfeit of silence come?—From the people who, for more than a century, entered so as not to be outside, and who, upon kneeling, terrified themselves with their own noise? From the silver pieces which, upon falling in the offertory box, lost their voices and utter only the smallest chirping of crickets when they are collected? Or from the comforting absence of Saint Anna, the sanctuary's patron saint, who does not dare to draw nearer for fear of spoiling the pure distance a prayer implies?

"Farfallettina"

Agitated, she arrives near the lamp and her vertigo gives her a final, muddled respite before she is incinerated. She collapses on the green tablecloth, and stretches out, for an instant against that flattering backdrop (for a span of time for her that we cannot measure), the luxury of her unimaginable splendor. One might say, in an understatement, that she resembles a woman who has a breakdown on her way to the Theater. She will never arrive there. Besides, what Theater caters to such a fragile audience . . . ? On her wings, we see flickers of gold moving like a double fan without a face to cover—between her wings, this slender body, a tumbler into which the emerald balls of two eyes fell. . . .

It's in you, my beauty, that God exhausted Himself. He throws you in the flames to regain a fraction of his power. (Like a child breaking his piggy bank).

The Eater of Mandarin Oranges

Oh what foresight! This, the rabbit-kind of fruits. Imagine! Thirty-seven little seeds in a single fruit, ready to fall everywhere and reproduce. We had to fix that. She, this little Mandarin, resolute, wearing a robe so large like she still wanted to grow, could have populated the earth. All in all, badly dressed, more concerned with multiplication than with fashion. Show her the pomegranate in its Cordovan leather armor: she explodes with newness, holds herself back, scorns . . . and allowing a glimpse of her future descendants, she suffocates them in a crimson cradle. To her, the earth seems too noncommittal to promise her abundance.

Maria Picone
Translated from the French of
Rainer Maria Rilke
1875 – 1926

Prose Poem

Beautiful landscape, embroidered with greenery, displayed tonight like a gorgeous silk in a merchant's display.

Petite goddess who continually hides herself under a cloak of water.

Birds that pass like a fleeting thought.

Country whose tragic expression forms from mixing the shadows of clouds.

Yet the green clarity of high mountain pastures gives them to the sky, rather than to the rugged peaks, concealed by fir trees, from which they form.

But the clouds have gaps in the sky of a sublimely distant blue, an infinite blue.

And to the West, behind other clouds, the violent setting of the sun seems to rupture itself on its hasty departure.

And always, facing me, the petite water goddess who dissolves and reemerges from her fall. The foam of her modesty, and the wave that remakes, again and again, her shoulder.

The grayness of a willow tree above her, and a wild rose with overflowing gestures that has bloomed for too long.

Maria Picone

Translated from the French of

Rainer Maria Rilke

1875 – 1926

Melon

Good melon, how are you so cool inside after requiring so much sun to grow? That reminds me of a sumptuous lover who had lips of spring, even at the apex of love's summer.

Maria Picone

Translated from the French of

Rainer Maria Rilke

1875 – 1926

Cemetery

Is there an aftertaste of life in these graves? Do the bees find, in the mouths of flowers, an almost-word which keeps silent? Oh flowers, prisoners to our instincts for happiness, do you return to us with our dead in your veins? How can you slip our grasp, flowers? How can you not be *our* flowers? Does the rose avoid us with all its petals? Can it become rose-only, nothing-but-rose? No one's sleep under so many eyelids?

John Ridland

Translated from the French of

Paul Valéry

1871 – 1942

The Seaside Cemetery at Sète

"Le Cimetière marin"

I

This peaceful roof, where dove-like sails parade,
Shimmers between the pines' and gravestones' shade;
Noon-on-the-dot displays there with its fires
The sea, the sea, always a new gestation!
Such a reward for such a contemplation
That gazing on the godlike calm inspires!

II

How the sheer energy, sharp and flashing, burns
So many diamonds the unseen foam upturns,
And such vast peacefulness seems to arise!
When the sun rests itself on the abyss,
The sheer, hard-laboring, infinite cause of this,
The Moment sparkles and the Dream is wise.

III

Treasure drum-tight, Minerva's simple temple,
Massively calm, an open storehouse, ample,
Of troublesome water, the Eye watches you fold
In somnolence, under a veil of flame,

My silence—O! Built up in the soul's name,
It fills, O Roof! a thousand tiles with gold!

IV

Temple of Time, a single sigh's concept,
At this pure point I strain to become adept,
All gathered in by gazing on the main;
And though I bring the gods my utmost offering,
Their scintillant serenity is scattering
Upon the depths a scathing royal disdain.

V

As fruit derives its essence from sensual pleasure,
When in delight it's gone, it meets its measure:
Inside a mouth is where its form disperses.
I breathe my future ashes, not entombed,
And heaven sings to the soul that is consumed
The shoreline's transformation, in murmuring verses.

VI

Heaven, true and beautiful, see how I change!
After such pride, and after so much strange
Idleness, with a plenitude of power,
I give myself to these bright shining spaces;
Over the homes of the dead my shadow paces,
Resigned to the frail brevity of my hour.

VII

Spirit exposed to the torches of the solstice,
I hold up to you, your admirable justice,

The gleam on weapons pity never made!
I give you back untouched your dominance:
Take note! . . . But to return the luminescence,
Suppose a morning half in lightless shade.

VIII

O for myself alone, on my own resources,
Keeping close to the heart, the poem's forces,
Between the chasm and the pure event,
I wait for the echo of my inner system,
Bitter, and dark, a sonorous cistern,
In the soul a future hollowly resonant.

IX

Do you know, apparent captive of the greenery,
You, Gulf, that gulps their fine-wire tracery,
I see the dazzling secrets with closed eyes;
What body drags me to its otiose death,
What seafront lures it to this bone-choked earth?
One spark and I think of my absent families.

X

Closed in and sacred, full of ethereal fire,
A plot of land that offers itself to its pyre,
I'm pleased by this place that's ruled by flaming torches,
Composed of gold and stone, funereal trees,
Where so much marble shivers in the shadows of these;
The faithful sea sleeps on my tombs' porches!

XI

Magnificent creature, spurning idolatry! while
I stand aloof, wearing a shepherd's smile,
And peer a long time at you, mysterious sheep,
At my tranquil tombs, a white flock against dark earth,
To which the prudent doves give a wide berth,
At the specious dreams inquisitive angels keep.

XII

Once arrived here, the future's dull and placid,
The tidy cicada scratches at the arid;
Everything's burnt, defunct, swept up in air,
With I-know-not-what severity of essence. . . .
Life is enormous, intoxicated on absence,
And bitterness is sweet, and the mind, clear.

XIII

The dead are happy, cached in this cemetery
Which warms them and dries up their mystery.
High Noon, motionless Noon, nothing can range,
Thinks out for itself its own inviolable space. . . .
At zenith, flawless diadem in place,
I am in you the secret force of change.

XIV

Only by me can your fears be constrained!
All I regret, and doubt, and have restrained,
Are your enormous diamond's imperfections. . . .
But in their night of marble ponderosities,
A vaguely human tribe at the roots of the trees
Already has joined your side, by slow defections.

XV

They are melted down to a thickness in the mind,
The red clay has drunk up their whiter kind,
Into the flowers the gift of life escapes!
Where are the familiar words they used to say,
The personal arts, their sole souls? Gone away.
The worm crawls in where their tears used to take shape.

XVI

The screeches of the teenagers being tickled,
The eyes, the teeth, the moistening of the eyelid,
The enchanting breast that flirts about with flame,
The blood that shines when lips return the kiss,
The final gift, fingers holding off this,
All go beneath the earth, and back to the game!

XVII

And you, great soul, are you longing for a dream
No longer tinted by colors that only seem,
Which the wave's gold light creates for bodily eyes?
Will you sing when you are merely vaporous?
Go on! All's fleeting! My being here is porous,
Your impatient supplication also dies!

XVIII

Frail immortality, gilt on black ground,
Consoler hideously laurel-crowned;
Which makes a breast of death, maternal, soft,
The lovely lie, and the reverential ruse!
Which doesn't know, and which does not refuse
This empty skull which has forever laughed!

XIX

Ancestors laid in earth, your heads thus filled,
Under the weight of so many spadefuls spilled,
You are the soil, confused by our tread above,
The veritable mole, worm irrefutable,
Do not scare you who sleep beneath the table,
They live off life, drawing mine away from love.

XX

Self-love, perhaps, or self-disgust, self-hate?
Its secret tooth draws nearer me of late,
So all these names are suitable to give!
And so? It sees, it dreams, it wants to touch!
My body pleases it, and on my couch,
I see I'm fitted thus to come alive!

XXI

Zeno! O cruel Zeno! Eleatic Zeno!
You've pierced me through and through with your fletched arrow
Which quivers, flies, and yet it does not fly!
The string's twang gives me birth, the arrow kills!
Ah! There's the sun. . . . What tortoise shadow thrills
The soul, Achilles' great stride standing by!

XXII

No, no! . . . Up, up! In life's successive storms!
Break down, my body, these over-thoughtful forms!
My lungs, breathe in the rebirth of the wind!
A freshness now being exhaled by the sea
Brings my soul back. . . . O salty energy!
Let's run to the waves, revived, and splash on in!

XXIII

Yes, mighty sea of insane genius,
A leopard's pelt and a cloak whose raggedness
Reflects from thousands of solar images,
Absolute hydra, drunk on your own blue flesh,
Biting your sparkling tail at every flash,
In a tumult wilder than its silences,

XXIV

The wind lifts! . . . We must try to live! And look:
The gigantic air opens and shuts my book,
Among the rocks, wave spume dares to spout out!
Blow away all my sun bedazzled pages!
Break, waves! Break, as the freshened water rages,
This tranquil roof where the jib-sails pecked about!

Translator's Note:

In the Larousse textbook of the original poem there is a rather awkward drawing by Valéry of the cemetery sloping down to the sea, which rises like the steep roof of the first stanza. (I have added the place-name to the poem's title in my translation.)

—*John Ridland*

Robert Schechter
Translated from the Danish of
Tove Ditlevsen
1917 – 1976

A Woman's Fear

("En Kvindes Frygt")

We're deeply in love, and everything's good.
To you all my days have been sworn.
But someday I fear you'll fall madly in love
with a woman who's yet to be born.

You tell me I'm sweet and you cover my mouth
with your kisses; I stroke your dark hair;
and yet in my heart I know time will replace
the joy I now feel with despair.

And what you now cherish and swear that you know
and kneel before, dream of and hold,
shall wither and fade, shrivel up for all time,
with even the memory grown cold.

You stare yourself blind in the luminous night
at my smooth, youthful face that beguiles,
but there in between us a lovely girl stands,
though I know you can't see her, who smiles.

She's younger than I am, the merest first note
of the song that still lives in the mind
of her mother, but someday she'll nest in your heart
and make you grow tipsy and blind.

There are men who must walk down a road without thought
and pick any rose that appears;
the happiest roses are those not yet born
and not to be picked yet for years.

But kneel down before me this minute. I'm young,
though it's brief as a butterfly's play.
Then kiss me and love me and toss me aside
among the plucked stems on your way.

I once loved a man with a heart just like yours,
and so, I don't care what you've sworn:
I tremble in fear of the power possessed
by a woman who's yet to be born.

Robert Schechter
Translated from the Spanish of
Sor Juana Inés de la Cruz
1648 – 1695

To Her Portrait

 This portrait that you see is painted fraud.
It uses art to show off beauty made
from syllogisms of both hue and shade
whose logic dupes the senses, but is flawed.

 This portrait, in which flattery contrives
to cancel out the ravages of time
and blur away the years beyond my prime,
to conquer age, decree that all survives,

 is hollow artifice contrived by care;
is a frail blossom that the wind has caught;
is useless as a charm against despair;

 is a fool's business, foolishly ill-wrought;
is wasted effort, and, if judgment's fair,
is corpse, is dust, is shadow, is pure naught.

Robert Schechter
Translated from the Spanish of
Sor Juana Inés de la Cruz
1648 – 1695

She'd Rather Die than Expose Herself to the Outrage of Growing Old

In the meadow, Celia spied a rose
that happily displayed the regal grace
produced by crimson makeup and by shows
of scarlet rouge that bathed its fragile face,

and said: "Enjoy, without a nod to fate,
the short span that's allowed your age of bloom,
since death tomorrow can't eliminate
the joy you live today, when it brings doom,

and though death may be hurrying to steal
your fragrant life away and leave you cold,
sorrow is not the emotion you should feel.

As those who learn from history are told,
it's luck to die when beauty still seems real
and you don't have to watch yourself grow old."

Wendy Sloan
Translated from the Italian of
Giacomo Leopardi
1798 – 1837

To Sylvia

"A Silvia"

Sylvia, do you still remember
that time of your mortal life
when beauty shined
from your laughing, elusive eyes
and you, with pensive grace,
approached the prime of youth?

The quiet rooms,
and the roads around, rang
with your perpetual song,
while you would sit, intent
on women's work, and so content
with vague daydreams about the days to come.
It was the month of May; you used
to spend your days that way.

I, sometimes putting aside
my books, the sweat-stained pages
where the best of my youth,
and of me, were spent,

and leaning from the veranda of my father's house
I'd prick up my ears at the sound of your voice,
and of your fast hands slapping the weary cloth.
I'd look out at the serene sky,
at the golden roads and the orchards,
on one side the sea, far-off, and on the other the mountains.
No mortal tongue can tell what I felt inside.

What soft thoughts,
what hopes, what hearts, oh, my Sylvia!
How they looked to us then,
human life and fate!
When I think of all that hope,
I'm oppressed by a feeling,
bitter and disconsolate,
and the pain of my misfortune comes back to me.
Why nature? Why?
Why don't you ever
make good on your promises?
Why deceive your children so?

You, before winter had withered the grass,
your fight with fatal illness lost,
lay dying, oh my tender one. And you didn't see
the full flower of your years;
your heart didn't melt
at the sweet praises now of your long black hair,
now of your shy, enamored glances.
Your friends never spent their Sundays
talking on with you all about love.

And before long
my own sweet hopes died too:
my years, my youth, too,
were cut off by the fates. Aye how,
how you passed away,
dear companion of my early days.
My tear-stained hope!
Is this that world? These
the delights, the love, the work, the times
we talked and talked about together?
Is this the destiny of humankind?

At the first glimpse of reality
you fell, poor thing, and with your hand
pointed out, in the distance,
cold death and a naked tomb.

A.E. Stallings
Translated from the Greek of
Hesiod
c. 8 BC

The Five Races of Man

(lines 109-201 of *Works and Days*)

The first race of humanity was Gold;
The Olympian gods created it of old,
In the time of Kronos, when he ruled the air.
Like gods they lived, with spirits free from care;
And grim old age never encroached. The feast
Where they moved limbs to music never ceased;
Their hands and feet not changing in the least.
They were free from every evil you could number,
And when death came, it stole on them like slumber.
They had good things galore; a bumper yield
Of corn sprung volunteering from the field.
They shared the harvest, easy as you please,
And gentle, willing, dwelt in peace and ease,
[Loved by the gods, their sheep crowding the fold.]
When earth had covered up this race of Gold,
As spirits they remained, by Zeus's will;
Benevolent, they move among us still,
Guardians who keep watch over men,
All justice and all crimes lie in their ken,
Shrouded with mist, they walk abroad in stealth,
And have in their gift the kingly boon of wealth.

The second race the gods made was by far
Inferior, a Silver Race, on par
In neither brains nor brawn: a child would cling,
Great baby, to his mother's apron string
A hundred years, playing house. And when in time
They came to puberty and reached their prime,
They did not live for long at all; instead
Their reckless acts of folly left them dead.
They had no self-control, could not restrain
Themselves from wreaking outrages and pain
On one another, counting among their vices
Neglect of the gods, the rightful sacrifices
That men perform, as custom says they must;
And then Zeus hid these also in disgust
Because they would not give the gods their due;
And so the ground has covered this race too;
And though they were inferior in worth,
Yet they are blessed shades beneath earth,
Honor attends them still. Then in their place
Zeus the Father forged a Brazen Race
Of men worse than the Silver; terrible, fierce
And tough as ash-wood for the hafts of spears:
War was their work—they loved the work of war—
The woeful deeds, the violence, the gore.
They ate no bread. Their hearts were hard as stone.
No one could touch them, for their might had grown
Great with their limbs. All weapons they would wield
Were bronze, their roofs were bronze, they worked the field

With tools of bronze, black iron unknown. They fell
At one another's hands to drafty Hell,
Nameless, for all their fearsomeness, undone
By death, snatched from the bright light of the sun.

And when the ground had covered up this race
In turn, Zeus made a Fourth one on the face
Of the richly battening earth, a juster one
And better, a god-like race of heroes known
As demi-gods—the race that came before
Our own on the boundless earth. These, wicked war
And the baneful battle-din laid low, one band
At Seven-gated Thebes, in Cadmus' land
Wrangling over Oedipus's sheep,
And others who sailed across the salty deep
To Troy, for Helen of the lovely hair.
And some the fate of death has buried there;
But others Zeus has settled near the tide
Of deep-swirled Ocean, to thrive there and abide
Far off from men—with spirits undistressed,
At the earth's ends, on Islands of the Blessed,
Happy heroes, for whom sweet fruits appear
And the fields yield their bounty thrice a year.

Would I were not among the Fifth. I'm torn:
Would I be better dead or not yet born?—
For this age is an Iron age indeed—
Suffering never ceases for our breed:
By day, men toil; night fritters them with care,

And the gods will give them troubles hard to bear;
But even so, some good things will alloy
Their lot of woe. Yet still, Zeus will destroy
This race, when babes are born already grey
At the temples, when a father in no way
Shall share a bond with sons, nor sons with father,
Nor guest with host, nor comrades with each other,
Nor brother love his brother as before;
Soon men won't honor parents anymore
But shall heap insults on old age—they'll learn
About the payback of the gods in turn—
Ingrates for their own rearing. Lacking pity,
With the rule of fist, one sacks another's city.
Thankless will be the man who keeps his word,
The good and the just. The wicked will be preferred
In honor, outrageous men who take the law
In their own hands, and there shall be no Awe.
The bad will harm the good; he won't be loath
To twist his words, and seal them with an oath.
And spiteful Envy, with her evil eye
And acid tongue shall keep herself close by
To every miserable man, while Awe
And Retribution shall indeed withdraw,
Abandoning mankind and the broad roads
Of the Earth, for the Olympian abodes
Of the Deathless Ones, veiling themselves in white
And hiding the beauty of their skin from sight.
Dismal troubles will be left behind;
No deliverance from evil for mankind.

A.E. Stallings
Translated from the Greek of
C.P. Cavafy
1863 – 1933

Interruption

It is we who interrupt the gods' work,
Rash beings of the moment, not from malice—
In Eleusis and in Phthia, in the palace,
Demeter and Thetis start on their sublime
Rites amidst tall flames and smoky murk.
But Metaneira bursts in on the scene
Each time, undone with terror; and each time
Peleus panics and will intervene.

Translator's Note:

This poem (rhymed in Greek), refers to two occasions in mythology where the gods were interrupted in the course of bestowing immortality on human infants. In the Homeric *Hymn to Demeter*, Demeter is in the midst of a rite to give prince Demophoon of Eleusis immortality (by burning the mortality out of him), when Queen Metaneira panics and interrupts her before the process is complete. Likewise, at least in Cavafy's version of the myth, the sea-nymph Thetis is in the midst of granting her son Achilles immortality when interrupted by his human father, Peleus, king of the Myrmidons in Phthia, Thessaly. (Traditionally, she dips Achilles in the river Styx to death-proof him, but because she is holding onto his eponymous heel, it remains his one vulnerable spot.)

—*A.E. Stallings*

Jeff Sypeck

Translated from the Latin of

Paul the Deacon

c. 720 – c. 799

Epitaph for the baby Hildegard, daughter of Charlemagne and Queen Hildegard

(9 May AD 783)

With bitter swiftness, death swept you away
As raw winds disperse spring's early blooms
Before life's first season; the light of a year
Will not glow for you. Little girl, you bequeathed us
No small sorrow when you sent your arrow
Right through the heart of your royal father.
Recalling your mother rekindled our grief;
You followed her by forty days.
In our world-bound hearts, we weep like rivers;
You exult and go forth, to faraway bliss.

N.S. Thompson
Translated from the Italian of
Giovanni Pascoli
1855 – 1912

October Evening

"Sera d'ottobre"

(from *Myricae*, 1892)

Along the roadside look what the hedgerow yields:
laughing groups of bright red berries; after plows
have worked, slowly to their mangers over fields
homeward come the cows.

A poor soul drags himself wearily along
through the brittle fallen leaves; sounding keener
than wind over fields, a girl sings her sad song
Fiore di spina![44]

---

44   *Fiore di spina* [flower of the thorn], a popular traditional folk song. Anna Magnani sings a coarser version in the title role of Pier Paolo Pasolini's film *Mamma Roma* (1962).

N.S. Thompson
Translated from the Italian of
Giovanni Pascoli
1855 – 1912

November

"Novembre"

(from *Myricae*, 1892)

The air is crystal clear, the sun so bright
that you look out for apricots in blossom
and in your heart you feel the bitter scents of white-
       thorn bending, lissom.

But like all greenery the thorn is dry
and the tread of feet makes a hollow sound
as bare black branches scar the empty sky
       over the barren ground.

Silence reigns; except in the wind you hear
from a distance the fragile fall of leaves
in gardens and plots of greens; summer, cold and clear,
       is both dead and grieves.

John Whitworth

Translated from the Greek of

Meleager

135 BC – 50 BC

Two Epigrams

i.

Tears for Heliodora
   I bring, a sorrow deep
As hell itself, with all
   My ruined love, to weep
For her small ghost among
   The ghosts on Acheron.
Where is my daffodil?
   Where is my pretty one?
Hades has her, dust
   And ashes on the blossom.
Earth, our mother, take her
   Gently to your bosom.

ii.

I picked a garland for
    My Heliodora, weaving
Snowdrop, laughing lily, soft
    Narcissus, interleaving
Myrtle, purple hyacinth,
    Sweet crocus, lovers' rose;
And she—a garland to my garland—
    Withering all those.

Ryan Wilson
Translated from the Spanish of
Lope de Vega
1562 – 1635

Tomorrow

"¿Qué tengo yo que mi amistad procuras?"

What do I have that You would be my friend?
What profit is there in it, Lord, for You,
That just outside my door, soaked by the dew,
You wait dark winter nights out to the end?

Oh, how hard my heart, for me to greet
You with a bolted door! Oh, what a rude
Madness if my chill ingratitude
Should freeze the bleeding wounds on Your pure feet!

So many times the angel said to me,
*Soul, look outside your window and you'll see
How lovingly He knocks, despite all sorrow.*

Oh sovereign beauty, how often did I say,
We'll open up the door for Him tomorrow,
Only to say the same the following day!

Ryan Wilson
Translated from the French of
Charles Baudelaire
1821 – 1897

Exotic Perfume

"Parfum Exotique"

When, with closed eyes, on a warm autumn night,
I breathe in deep the fragrance of your breast,
I see unrolling happy shorelines, blessed
With dazzling fires of an unchanging light—

An isle of indolence that nature supplies
With unfamiliar trees and fruits of rare
Savor; the men are lean and rugged there;
The women shock one with their brazen eyes.

Led by your scent into enchanted climes,
I see a harbor filled with sails and masts
Still worn out by the ocean's waves and blasts,

Meanwhile, the smell of bright green tamarinds
Is carried to the nose by circling winds
And merges in my soul with sailors' rhymes.

Translator's Note:

"Exotic Perfume" was dedicated by Baudelaire to his mistress, Jeanne Duval, a Haitian dancer and actress with whom he maintained a relationship for two decades. The sonnet appeared in his magnum opus, *Les Fleurs du mal,* which was published in 1857.

—*Ryan Wilson*

Shifra Zisman and *Laine Zisman Newman*
Translated from the Yiddish of
Dovid Zisman
1914 – 1960

A Spark of Freedom

See the sun
It shines
Its light, so bright.
In Buchenwald, the concentration camp
You are here.
No, it won't always be this way.
I see a spark of freedom.
It clangs out the hour.

So many corpses.
Remember this well!
Every tree is a witness.
Barbwire without pity,
But it is enough!

Hear through the distance, bells sound.
They sing out a song:
The Song of Freedom.

Do you hear the music?
Yes. I hear the song that calls me
It says come, fast, faster, fight!
Because that is where my luck lies.

From prisons open gates, open doors.
Come all. Come out with me.
Gathering in streets, masses, with a song
To fight! We are ready!
Arise from the ovens with fists clenched!
Now is the time!

Fighting between races,
End at once! It's enough!
The righteous and the free
In the world will know.

We are together amidst the flames
We are building a new world
Of good people
Of free people.

AbleMUSE
A REVIEW OF POETRY, PROSE & ART

After more than a decade of online publishing excellence, Able Muse began a bold new chapter with its print edition

We continue to bring you in print the usual masterful craft with poetry, fiction, essays, art & photography, and book reviews

Check out our 12+ years of online archives for work by

RACHEL HADAS • X.J. KENNEDY • TIMOTHY STEELE • MARK JARMAN • A.E. STALLINGS • DICK DAVIS • A.M. JUSTER • TIMOTHY MURPHY • DEBORAH WARREN • CHELSEA RATHBURN • RHINA P. ESPAILLAT • TURNER CASSITY • RICHARD MOORE • STEPHEN EDGAR • ANNIE FINCH • THAISA FRANK • NINA SCHUYLER • SOLITAIRE MILES • MISHA GORDIN • & SEVERAL OTHERS

SUBSCRIPTION
Able Muse - Print Edition - Subscriptions:

Able Muse is published semiannually.
Subscription rates for individuals: $24.00 per year; single and previous issues: $16.95 + $3 S&H.
International subscription rate: $33 per year; single and previous issues: $16.95 + $5 S&H.
(All rates in USD.)

Subscribe online with PayPal/credit card **www.ablemusepress.com**

Or send a check payable to *Able Muse Review*
Attn: Alex Pepple - Editor, Able Muse, 467 Saratoga Avenue #602, San Jose, CA 95129 USA

Credo for the Checkout Line in Winter

Poems
by Maryann Corbett

NEW ~ from Able Muse Press

Finalist, 2011 Able Muse Book Award

PRAISE FOR *CREDO* . . .
(with a Foreword by Peter Campion)

The second collection of original poetry from Maryann Corbett

★★★★★

*"She is a newborn Robert Frost,
with a wicked eye for contemporary life."*
— Willis Barnstone

*"[She] remains a poet of the first order, and her
poems are cause for gratitude, and deep enjoyment."*
— Peter Campion (from the foreword)

*"A stunning collection, from one of America's
most gifted contemporary poets."*
— Marilyn L. Taylor

"Sharply visual, skillfully and cleverly crafted."
— Catharine Savage Brosman

*"Corbett is one of the best-kept secrets
of American poetry, and this is
one of the best new collections I've read in years."*
— Geoffrey Brock

ISBN 978-1-927409-14-5 / 102 pages

ORDER NOW FROM ABLE MUSE PRESS AT: WWW.ABLEMUSEPRESS.COM
OR, ORDER FROM AMAZON.COM, BN.COM, . . . & OTHER ONLINE OR OFFLINE BOOKSTORES

www.AbleMusePress.com

Pumpkin Chucking

Poems

by Stephen Scaer

NEW~ from Able Muse Press

Finalist, 2012 Able Muse Book Award

PRAISE FOR *PUMPKIN CHUCKING*
(with a Foreword by A.M. Juster)

The first full-length collection from Stephen Scaer

★★★★★

"... the prevailing voice in this collection belongs to a hugely entertaining, middle-aged, middle-class Everyman writing about the everyday."
— Deborah Warren

"Stephen Scaer's Pumpkin Chucking celebrates the New England landscape while still being universal ... with wit in the winking way of Frost."
— A.M. Juster (from the foreword)

"... a tour of the expressive possibilities of all of English poetry"
— Richard Wakefield

"This is a wonderful and entertaining book of poetry."
— Robert Crawford

ISBN 978-1-927409-12-1 / 90 pages

ORDER NOW FROM ABLE MUSE PRESS AT: WWW.ABLEMUSEPRESS.COM
OR, ORDER FROM AMAZON.COM, BN.COM, ... & OTHER ONLINE OR OFFLINE BOOKSTORES

www.AbleMusePress.com

The Dark Gnu and Other Poems
written & illustrated by Wendy Videlock

*NEW~ *from* Able Muse Press

The Second Full-Length Collection of Poetry from Wendy Videlock

★★★★★

"Wendy Videlock's poems contain laughing pears, rhyming coyotes, and jaded wind. In reading this book, I found myself laughing and gasping in equal measures. And cursing, as well, because Videlock is so damn good and I'm so damn jealous of her talent. She is one of my very favorite poets."
— Sherman Alexie

"Reminiscent in some ways of Shel Silverstein's classic collections, Videlock's new book, The Dark Gnu and Other Poems, supplements shy whimsy with mystery and a hint of tragedy. These poems remind readers "of all inconceivable ages" that not all problems have solutions and that some narratives end in mystery rather than in resolution. The Dark Gnu *is enhanced by the author's illustrations that deepen the allure of the poems."*
— Jeremy Telman

ISBN 978-1-927409-09-1 / 96 pages (paperback)
ISBN 978-1-927409-13-8 / 94 pages (Deluxe Edition - hardcover)
ORDER NOW FROM ABLE MUSE PRESS AT: WWW.ABLEMUSEPRESS.COM
OR, ORDER FROM AMAZON.COM, BN.COM, ... & OTHER ONLINE OR OFFLINE BOOKSTORES

www.AbleMusePress.com

COMING SOON
2014 / 2015
from

Able Muse Press

William Baer, *Times Square and Other Stories*

William Conelly, *Uncontested Grounds - Poems*

John Drury, *Sea Level Rising - Poems*

D.R. Goodman, *Greed: A Confession - Poems*

Martin McGovern, *Bad Fame - Poems*

Jeredith Merrin, *Cup - Poems*

Richard Newman, *All the Wasted Beauty of the World - Poems*

Wendy Videlock, *Only an Echo - Poems*

Chelsea Woodard, *Vellum - Poems*

MORE INFORMATION AVAILABLE AT

www.AbleMusePress.com

~ from Able Muse Press

This Bed Our Bodies Shaped
Poems
by April Lindner

Life in the Second Circle
Poems
by Michael Cantor

SHORTLISTED BOOK, 2013
MASSACHUSETTS BOOK AWARD

"All the pleasures and pains of domestic life, of marriage and parenthood, love and loss, dailiness and major rites of passage, find their textures and music in the poems of April Lindner's new collection."
— Mark Jarman

"Like Muhammad Ali, one of the 'Box Men' he celebrates in a virtuosic crown of sonnets, Cantor is a master of floating like a butterfly in a small, roped-off space."
— Catherine Tufariello

www.AbleMusePress.com

~ from **Able Muse Press**

The Cosmic Purr
Poems
by Aaron Poochigian

A Vertical Mile
Poems
by Richard Wakefield

"A major translator from classical Greek, Poochigian offers in his own poetry a hip formality, a timeless sense of the contemporary."
— David Mason

"As a poet of the outdoors—one who sees and, seeing, makes new what he has seen— Wakefield is unsurpassed."
— R.S. Gwynn

www.AbleMusePress.com

Grasshopper:
The Poetry of M A Griffiths

~ Now reprinted & distributed in the USA & Canada by **Able Muse Press**

Grasshopper

The Poetry of
M A Griffiths

Margaret Ann Griffiths (1947-2009)

Margaret was born and raised in London and lived for some time in Bracknell then later moved to Poole. Rather than seek publication through traditional channels, she was content to share her work with fellow poets on various Internet forums. On the rare occasions she submitted work for publication, it was typically to online venues. Also known by the Internet pseudonyms "Grasshopper" and "Maz," she began posting her poetry online in 2001. During the mid-2000s she worked from home, running a small Internet-based business, and edited the *Poetry Worm*, a monthly periodical distributed by email.

In 2008, her "Opening a Jar of Dead Sea Mud" won *Eratosphere*'s annual Sonnet Bake-off, and was praised by Richard Wilbur. Later that year she was a Guest Poet on the Academy of American Poets website, where she was hailed as "one of the up-and-coming poets of our time."

She suffered for years from a stomach ailment which eventually proved fatal in July 2009. Almost immediately after her death was announced on *Eratosphere*, poets from all over the English-speaking world, from London, Derby, Scotland, Wales, Queensland, New South Wales, Massachusetts, New York, Minnesota, Missouri, Maryland, California and Texas collected her work for this publication.

▫ First published by Arrowhead Press in the UK (January, 2011)
▫ Reprinted and distributed in the USA and Canada by Able Muse Press (April, 2011)

ISBN 978-1-904852-28-5 / 384 pages
ORDER NOW FROM ABLE MUSE PRESS AT: WWW.ABLEMUSEPRESS.COM
OR, ORDER FROM AMAZON.COM, BN.COM, . . . & OTHER ONLINE OR OFFLINE BOOKSTORES

www.AbleMusePress.com

Able Muse - Winter 2012
Print Edition, No. 14

WITH THE 2012 ABLE MUSE WRITE PRIZE FOR POETRY & FICTION

Includes the winning story and poems from the 2012 contest winners and finalists.

FEATURED ARTIST
Nicolas Evariste

FEATURED POET
Catherine Tufariello
(Interviewed by Uche Ogbuji)

★★★★★

POETRY, FICTION, BOOK REVIEWS, INTERVIEWS & ESSAYS FROM CATHARINE SAVAGE BROSMAN   THOMAS CARPER   LORNA KNOWLES BLAKE   RICHARD WAKEFIELD   TIMOTHY MURPHY   KATHRYN LOCEY   TONY BARNSTONE   LEN KRISAK   LEWIS BUZBEE   EVELYN SOMERS   GIGI MARK   GREGORY DOWLING   MICHAEL COHEN   PETER BYRNE   AARON POOCHIGIAN   AND OTHERS

212 pages
ISBN 978-1-927409-07-7

ORDER NOW FROM ABLE MUSE PRESS AT: WWW.ABLEMUSEPRESS.COM
OR, ORDER FROM AMAZON.COM, BN.COM, ... & OTHER ONLINE OR OFFLINE BOOKSTORES

www.AbleMusePress.com

Able Muse - Summer 2013
Print Edition, No. 15

WITH POETRY • FICTION • ESSAYS • BOOK REVIEWS • ART & PHOTOGRAPHY

FEATURED ARTIST
Clara Lieu
(Interviewed by Sharon Passmore)

FEATURED POET
Greg Williamson
(Interviewed by Stephen Kampa)

★★★★★

POETRY, FICTION, BOOK REVIEWS, INTERVIEWS & ESSAYS FROM DICK ALLEN FRED LONGWORTH CATHARINE SAVAGE BROSMAN ROBERT J. LEVY LEN KRISAK CALLIE SISKEL D.R. GOODMAN HALEY HACH TIMOTHY MURPHY RAY NAYLER ROBERT SCHULTZ ILYA LYASHEVSKY RYAN WILSON DAVID MASON PETER BYRNE DAVID CAPLAN STEPHEN KAMPA DEREK FURR N.S. THOMPSON AND OTHERS

142 pages
ISBN 978-1-927409-21-3

ORDER NOW FROM ABLE MUSE PRESS AT: WWW.ABLEMUSEPRESS.COM
OR, ORDER FROM AMAZON.COM, BN.COM, ... & OTHER ONLINE OR OFFLINE BOOKSTORES

www.AbleMusePress.com

RIDDLE NOTES

"Riddles" on page 105:
    1. *death*
    2. *mirror*

"Riddles" on page 110:

    1. *rainbow*
    2. *shadow*

CONTRIBUTOR NOTES

DELMIRA AGUSTINI was born on October 24, 1886, in Montevideo, Uruguay. She began to publish her work at an early age, and in her short life published three volumes of poetry: *El libro blanco (Frágil)* [The White Book—Fragile] (1907), *Cantos de la mañana* [Morning Songs] (1910), and *Los calices vacíos* [The Empty Chalices] (1913). An early *modernista*, Agustini was influenced both by the French Parnassians and the French symbolists. Her passionate and sensual work, which challenged the social conventions of the day, was highly praised by poets such as María Eugenia Vaz Ferreira, Julio Herrera y Reissig, Leopoldo Lugones, and Rubén Darío . She had planned on publishing a fourth book, *Los astros del abismo* [Stars of the Abyss], but was murdered by her ex-husband in July of 1914. These poems were subsequently included in her *Obras completas,* consisting of two volumes: *El rosario de Eros* [The Rosary of Eros] and *Los astros del abismo,* published posthumously in 1924. This year marks the one hundredth anniversary of the death of Delmira Agustini, considered as one of the preeminent women poets of Latin America.

DANTE ALIGHIERI (1265 – 1321) is widely regarded as one of the world's greatest poets. His *Vita Nova* (c. 1292 – 95), a combination of prose and poetry that tells the story of his youthful love for Beatrice, was his first book. In 1295 he entered Florentine politics and in the summer of 1300 he became one of the six governing Priors of Florence, the highest political office. During this time, he was also writing the numerous lyric poems that made him famous in central and northern Italy, as well as studying widely and deeply in a number of subjects. In 1302, the political situation forced Dante and his party into exile. For the rest of his life he depended for refuge on the generosity of various courts in northern Italy. He continued to write, producing two unfinished works—the first treatise of literary criticism (*De vulgari eloquentia* [On Eloquence in the Vernacular]) and the first treatise of philosophy (the *Convivio* [Banquet]) in a European vernacular language—before starting his work on *The Divine Comedy.* At some point late in life he took asylum in Ravenna, where he completed *The Divine Comedy.* He died, probably from malaria, soon after having returned to Ravenna from a diplomatic mission in Venice.

CECCO ANGIOLIERI (c. 1260 – c. 1312), the son of a banker father and noblewoman mother, lived in Siena and wrote roughly 110 sonnets. He sometimes found himself in legal and financial troubles, and upon his death he left an indebted estate to his children. At some point he met Dante, possibly when both were involved in Siena's and Florence's alliance against Arezzo in the Battle of Campaldino (1289). Three of Angiolieri's sonnets to Dante exist, perhaps as a part of a *tenzone* or poets' exchange. (Dante's responses, if he made them, are unfortunately lost.) As the sonnets featured here attest, he often wrote about love's cruelties and the hardship of being broke, lamenting in one poem the sturdy health of his father and thus the distant prospects of his inheritance. Dante Gabriel Rossetti first translated some of Angiolieri's poems into English, and critically he is often identified with a "comic-realistic" school of medieval Italian poetry, which parodied and deflated the courtliness and philosophical high-mindedness of the *dolce stil nuovo* poets.

AYESHEH-YE AFGHAN, a late 18th- / early 19th-century poet who as a young woman was a member of the court of Taymur Shah Duranni, was the most successful of the 18th-century Afghan monarchs. Famous in her own lifetime, she is the most significant Afghan woman poet to have written in Persian; she wrote both secular and mystical poems in most of the genres of classical Persian verse. Her elegies for her son, killed during a war in Kashmir, are particularly admired.

WILLIAM BAER, a recent Guggenheim fellow, is the author of sixteen books including *Selected Sonnets: Luís de Camões* (University of Chicago Press, 2005). A former Fulbright Professor at the University of Coimbra in Portugal, his translations from the Portuguese, Spanish, and Italian have been published in *The London Review, New Letters, Atlanta Review, First Things, Portuguese Literary & Cultural Studies, Modern Poetry in Translation,* and other periodicals.

NED BALBO's latest book, *The Trials of Edgar Poe and Other Poems,* was awarded the 2010 Donald Justice Prize and the 2012 Poets' Prize. *Lives of the Sleepers* received the Ernest Sandeen Prize and a *ForeWord* Book of the Year Gold Medal; *Galileo's Banquet* shared the Towson University Prize. A selection of poems based on the paintings of Nora Sturges appears in the 2012 *Avatar Review,* and variations on poems by Apollinaire, Baudelaire, Rilke, Rimbaud, Trakl, and Valéry are out or forthcoming in *Birmingham Poetry Review, Bluestem, Evansville Review, String Poet, Unsplendid,* and elsewhere. He is co-winner of the 2013 Willis Barnstone Translation Prize.

TONY BARNSTONE is The Albert Upton Professor and Chair of English at Whittier College and author of fifteen books and a music CD, *Tokyo's Burning: WWII Songs*. His poetry books include *Beast in the Apartment, Tongue of War: From Pearl Harbor to Nagasaki, The Golem of Los Angeles, Sad Jazz: Sonnets, Impure,* and selected poems in Spanish, *Buda en Llamas: Antología poética (1999-2012)*. He is also a distinguished translator of Chinese literature, and he dabbles in other languages. In 2014 – 15 he'll publish two anthologies: *Dead and Undead Poems* and *Human and Inhuman Monstrous Verse* and a seventh book of poems. Selected honors include prizes from the NEA, California Arts Council, Poets Prize, Pushcart, Strokestown International, John Ciardi, and Benjamin Saltman.

WILLIS BARNSTONE was born in Lewiston, Maine, and educated at Bowdoin, the Sorbonne, the School of Oriental and African Studies at the University of London, Columbia and Yale, taught in Greece at the end of the civil war (1949 – 1951), in Buenos Aires during the Dirty War, and during the Cultural Revolution he went to China, where he was later a Fulbright Professor at Beijing Foreign Studies University (1984 – 1985). A former O'Connor Professor of Greek at Colgate University, he is Distinguished Professor Emeritus of Comparative Literature and Spanish at Indiana University. The author of some seventy books with university and trade presses, he is publishing *ABC of Translation* (Black Widow Press) in March 2014 and *Borges at Eighty* (New Directions) in May. Carcanet in England will published his *Selected Poems*.

CHARLES BAUDELAIRE (1821 – 1897) holds the most wide-ranging influence of the French Symbolist poets. A respected reviewer and critic whose translations of Edgar Allan Poe were much admired in his time, he died young, at only forty-six, but left behind a legacy of work at the center of which stands his masterpiece, the poems of *Les Fleurs du mal*, first published in 1857 to shock and acclaim. (Victor Hugo was an admirer, as were Rimbaud, Verlaine, and others.) Baudelaire's prosodic confidence, deft use of rhyme, and absolute control of tone provide a striking contrast with the tumultuous emotional life that his poems record. Particularly impressive are his imaginative range and insight into the human psyche as he observed it in the urban life of Paris.

MARK S. BAUER's poems have appeared in various literary journals and two chapbooks: *Imperial Days* (Robert Barth Publishing, 2002), a chapbook of epigrams, and *The Gnarled Man Rises* (Scienter Press, 2005), a chapbook of lyrics. He edited the anthology *A Mind Apart: Poems of Melancholy, Madness, & Addiction* (Oxford, 2009), and is on the psychiatry faculty at Harvard Medical School.

MICHAEL BRADBURN-RUSTER, a native of Carmel, California, has published poetry, fiction, translations, and scholarly essays in international journals including *Able Muse, Sacred Web, Cincinnati Review, Grey Sparrow Journal, Perigee, Broken Bridge Review, Marginalia, Berkeley Poetry Review, Rain City Review, Damazine* (Syria), and *Antigonish Review*. He is a frequent contributor to *Poetry Salzburg Review*, and was a featured reader at the Monterey Bay Poetry Festival. Since receiving a doctorate from UC Berkeley, he has taught literature, philosophy, comparative religions and mythology in California, Oregon, and Arizona. His book *The Angel or the Beast* (1998) explored the interplay of philosophy, mysticism, theology and literature in the Spanish Renaissance. His translation of the award-winning Spanish novel *Lady of the South Wind* was published by (the now sadly mythical) North Point Press.

BERTOLT BRECHT (1898 – 1956) was a German playwright and poet. A dedicated Marxist, Brecht is perhaps best known for helping to develop the theatrical movement known as epic theater, which considered the stage a medium for exploring political ideas and dialectical materialism. Over his lifetime, Brecht wrote two books of fiction, multiple theoretical works on theatre, over fifty plays, and hundreds of poems. He composed *"Vom ertrunkenen Mädchen"* [Of the Drowned Girl] after the brutal murder of revolutionary Rosa Luxemburg during the Spartacist Uprising of 1919.

Gaius Valerius Catullus (c. 84 BC – 54 BC) was a Latin poet of the late Roman Republic whose work had a profound influence on later Latin poets, including Ovid, Horace, and Virgil. Approximately 116 of Catullus's often-translated poems have survived.

C.P. Cavafy (1863 – 1933) is the most famous and arguably greatest of the Modern Greek Poets. He was born and died in Alexandria, but spent part of his childhood in Liverpool (his first poems were in English and he is said to have spoken Greek with an English accent), and he lived for a time in Constantinople. His subjects range from homosexual love affairs to arcane Hellenistic history, but his treatments of them share a remove in time, a distance or irony. His poems were collected only after his death. Many celebrations this past year have marked the sesquicentennial of his birth.

Catherine Chandler was born in New York City, grew up in Wilkes-Barre, Pennsylvania, and currently lives in Saint-Lazare, Quebec, and Punta del Este, Uruguay. She is the author of two full-length collections of poetry, *Lines of Flight* (Able Muse Press, 2011) and *Glad and Sorry Seasons* (Biblioasis, 2014), a collection of sonnets, *This Sweet Order* (White Violet Press, 2012) and two chapbooks, *For No Good Reason* and *All or Nothing*. She lectured in Spanish at McGill University's Department of Translation Studies for many years and also acted as McGill's International Affairs Officer for Latin America. She also taught Spanish at Concordia University's Language Institute. Winner of the Howard Nemerov Sonnet Award and *The Lyric* quarterly award, her poetry, essays and literary translations from French and Spanish have appeared in numerous print and online journals and anthologies throughout the English-speaking world. Recently retired, Catherine teaches English as a Second Language and Music in the Commission scolaire des Trois-Lacs.

Christine de Pizan (1364 – c. 1430) was the daughter of the official astrologer to the French court, who gave her the same education that a son would have received. When her husband died of plague, leaving her a widow with three children at the age of 25, she began a career of writing, both prose and poetry, which marks her as a first European woman to support herself entirely by her pen. She enjoyed the patronage of the court and the nobility for her poetic works; the most famous of these are the poems that mourn the death of her husband, but she explores all aspects of courtly love and courtly behavior. She is probably best known for *The Book of the City of Ladies* and *The Treasure of the City of Ladies,* prose works in which she defended the position of women from the misogynist views that were common in her day.

Terese Coe's poems and translations have appeared in *Poetry, The Threepenny Review, Ploughshares, New American Writing, Alaska Quarterly Review, The Cincinnati Review, Smartish Pace, Tar River Poetry* and *The Huffington Post*; in the UK, *The TLS, Poetry Review, Agenda, New Walk Magazine, Orbis,* and *Warwick Review*; in Ireland, *The Stinging Fly*; and in many other publications, including anthologies. She has written several plays, including *Harry Smith at the Chelsea Hotel*, about the celebrated collector of *The Anthology of American Folk Music,* filmmaker, and wit. Copies of her poem "More" were heli-dropped across London as part of the 2012 London Olympics' Poetry Parnassus.

Maryann Corbett's third book of poetry, *Mid Evil,* won the 2014 Richard Wilbur Award and is forthcoming from The Evansville Press. Her poems, essays, reviews, and translations have appeared widely in journals in print and online and in a variety of anthologies and have also won the Lyric Memorial Award and the Willis Barnstone Translation Prize. Recent work appears in *32 Poems, Modern Poetry in Translation, Light, Barrow Street, Southwest Review, Verse Daily,* and *American Life in Poetry.* Her two previous books are *Breath Control* and *Credo for the Checkout Line in Winter,* a finalist for the Able Muse Book Award.

José Corredor-Matheos (b. 1929) graduated with a degree in law, but never practiced, working instead as editor for the publishing house Espasa-Calpa. He is known as a poet and art critic. He has published multiple books of poetry, most recently *Desolación y vuelo, Poesía reunida* (2011), and has received numerous awards: the Premio Boscán de Poesía for *Poema para un nuevo libro* in 1961, the Premio Nacional de Poesía for *El don de la ignorancia* in 2005, and the Cuidad de Barcelona prize for *Un pez que va por el jardín* in 2008. His translations won him the Premio Nacional de Traducción entre Lenguas Españolas for the bilingual anthology of *Poesía catalane contemporánea* in 1984. He also has published work on contemporary art, architecture, and design, for which he won the 1993 Premi d'Arts Plàstiques from the Generalitat de Cataluña, the Medalla de Oro of the Ayuntamiento de Barcelona, and was honored as Académico Correspondiente of the Real Academia de Belles Artes of San Fernando and Académico de Honor of the Real Academia de Bellas Artes of San Jorge. He lives in Barcelona.

Heidi Czerwiec is Associate Professor of English and Creative Writing at the University of North Dakota, and is the author of *Self-Portrait as Bettie Page* (Barefoot Muse, 2013). Her poems and translations are published or forthcoming in *Angle, storySouth, Crab Orchard Review,* and *International Poetry Review.*

Dick Davis is Professor Emeritus of Persian at Ohio State University, where he was chair of the Department of Near Eastern Languages and Cultures from 2002 to 2012. He has written scholarly works on both English and Persian literature, as well as eight volumes of his own poetry. His publications include volumes of poetry and verse translation chosen as books of the year by *The Sunday Times* (UK), 1989; *The Daily Telegraph* (UK), 1989; *The Economist* (UK), 2002; *The Washington Post,* 2010, and *The Times Literary Supplement* (UK), 2013. He has published numerous book-length verse translations from medieval Persian, most recently, *Faces of Love: Hafez and the Poets of Shiraz* (2012), and has been called, by the *Times Literary Supplement,* "our finest translator from Persian." He is currently translating work by Persian woman poets, from the beginnings in the 10th century to the present day, with a view to producing an anthology of their poems.

Tove Ditlevsen (1917 – 1976) was a Danish author of deeply personal and heartfelt stories, novels and memoirs, though she considered herself primarily a poet. Married four times, she struggled with substance abuse and mental illness throughout her life. She committed suicide in 1976.

Gavin Douglas (c. 1474 – 1522) represented, along with William Dunbar and Robert Henryson, the flowering of the golden age of the Northern Renaissance in Scotland. Douglas studied for the priesthood and traveled widely, absorbing both contemporary and classical virtues and resources. Completed in 1513, his monumental translation of Virgil's *Aeneid* was the first complete verse rendition of a classical text to be produced in Scotland. Later in life, Douglas became Bishop of Dunkeld and tutor to the young James V, involving himself entirely in political rather than literary affairs and intrigues. He concluded his years in exile in England, where he died of the plague. The excerpt given here from Book 7 of *Eneados* lavishly demonstrates Douglas' capacity for elaborating upon the details and designs glossed or implied within Virgil's text while still remaining true to the letter and spirit of the original; a master of the microcosm within the macrocosm, Douglas expands rather than exaggerates upon the Virgilian base.

William Dunbar (c. 1456 – 1520) trained as a Franciscan novice in addition to studying at the University of St Andrews, Oxford, and Paris. He served as an ambassador and court poet of King James IV, for whom his work epitomized the ideals of the "Northern Renaissance." His most famous work, "Lament for the Makaris" eulogizes twenty-four early Scots/English poets including Geoffrey Chaucer, John Barbour, Blind Harry, and Robert Henryson. As "*The Twa Cummeris*" illustrates, however, Dunbar was equally comfortable dipping his quill in bile as in tears, and proved one of Scotland's great comic as well as dramatic poets.

Adam Elgar's poems have appeared in a range of journals including *Poetry Review, Stand, Warwick Review, Magma, Orbis,* and *Iota*. He also translates verse and prose from Italian and French. The novelist and scientist Alessandra Lavagnino is collaborating with him on the complete translation of her work. His version of her novella *Truth and Flies* is published by Troubador Storia, and her short stories have appeared in *Stand* and *New Walk* magazines in Elgar's translations. He has recently collaborated with the poet Valerio Magrelli on a set of sonnets for the Italian Cultural Institute in London *(A Sentimental History of a Restoration*, Alma Classics).

His ongoing translation of the complete Don Camillo stories by Giovanni Guareschi is published by Pilot Productions. He translates for *The International Journal of Psychoanalysis* and the Vatican Museums, and until 2013 was the Translation moderator at *Able Muse*'s online literary forum *Eratosphere*.

Euripides (480 BC – 406 BC) was the youngest of the three great Athenian tragedians whose work survives. From the voluminous number of tragedies these three playwrights produced, we have seven apiece by Aeschylus and Sophocles, and eighteen or nineteen by Euripides, who was called in antiquity the most tragic of the tragic poets, and of whom it was also said that he showed people not as they ought to be but as they are. Some of the ancient references to Euripides, while they can't be substantiated, give a vivid sense of the nature and popularity of his art. For example, Plutarch tells us that the dire failure of the Sicilian Expedition late in the Peloponnesian War led Athenians who had been enslaved in Syracuse to trade renditions of passages they recalled from Euripidean tragedies with their Sicilian captors in exchange for food and drink. Euripides also makes several appearances in the comedies of Aristophanes, most memorably in *The Frogs*, where he loses the dead tragic poets' contest to Aeschylus but emerges as the more humane, realistic, and finally sympathetic personality and artist.

BRETT FOSTER is the author of two poetry collections, *The Garbage Eater* (Triquarterly Books/Northwestern University Press) and *Fall Run Road*, which was awarded Finishing Line Press's Open Chapbook Prize. His translations of Cecco Angiolieri's sonnets have appeared in numerous italianate publications and literary journals, including *Italian Poetry Review, Journal of Italian Translation, Yale Italian Poetry, Green Mountains Review, Metamorphoses, Smartish Pace, Tupelo Quarterly,* and *Unsplendid*. One poem was awarded the Willis Barnstone Translation Prize, and appeared in *The Evansville Review*. A recipient of a PEN American Center translation grant, he is close to completing *Elemental Rebel: The* Rime *of Cecco Angiolieri,* a selected volume of Angiolieri's poetry in English.

WILLIAM FOWLER (1560 – 1612) was a Protestant spy in Paris before returning to Scotland to become a minister and, later, moving to London to serve as secretary to Queen Anne. Besides composing original work, he also translated widely from the Italian masters such as Petrarch and Castiglione. His "Sonet: In Orknay" utilizes the rhyme scheme popularized by Fowler's English contemporary, Edmund Spenser (1552 – 1599), thus representing Fowler's quick talent for absorbing both classical and current trends in literature.

ANDREW FRISARDI is originally from Boston and now lives in northern Lazio, Italy, where he works as a writer, translator, and editor. His most recent books are an annotated translation of Dante's *Vita Nova*, published by Northwestern University Press in 2012; *The Young Dante and the One Love,* essays on the *Vita Nova* published by the Temenos Academy (London) in 2013; and *Death of a Dissembler,* a poetry collection published in 2014 by White Violet Press. He is currently at work on an annotated translation of Dante's *Convivio,* for which he was awarded a Guggenheim Fellowship in 2013.

DIANE FURTNEY, after her Tulsa upbringing and with a psychology degree from Vassar College, worked a year in Israel (1967), then took an assortment of jobs, sometimes in clinical psychology, in several US cities. Besides nonfiction ghostwriting, she has authored two prizewinning poetry chapbooks *(Destination Rooms* and *It Was a Game)* and two comic mystery novels (pseudonym D.J.H. Jones). Her poems and translations (French, Japanese) are in numerous journals in the US and England, including *The Virginia Quarterly Review, The Iowa Review, Poetry International, Circumference* and *Stand*. A full-length collection of science-based poems, *Science And,* was published in 2014 by FutureCycle Press. She now lives with her spouse, near Phoenix.

GÉRARD DE NERVAL (1808 – 1855) was one of several pseudonyms used by Gérard Labrunie, who translated Goethe's *Faust* at age 19 and continued to import German Romanticism into French while also reverting to Renaissance poets for sonnet forms. A theater critic, travel writer and prose stylist, he is also ranked, on the basis of a dozen evocative sonnets, as one of the finest French poets. Subject to repeated schizophrenic breakdowns, he died at 47. His last words, in a note to his aunt on a winter afternoon before he hanged himself, were "Don't wait up for me tonight, for the night will be black and white."

ASADULLAH KHAN GHALIB (1797 – 1869), known by his pen name, Ghalib, is the famous romantic and mystical poet of the Mughal Empire in India. His poems are characterized by great wit, puns, and a mystical, erotic imagery so passionate as to veer at times into the surreal. He is the acknowledged world master of the ghazal, though certain Persian poets such as Hafiz and Rumi give him a run for his money!

RACHEL HADAS is Board of Governors Professor of English at the Newark campus of Rutgers University. The most recent of her many books of poems is *The Golden Road* (Northwestern University Press, 2012); a memoir, *Strange Relation,* was published by Paul Dry Books in 2011. In preparation now are a book of prose pieces, *Talking to the Dead,* forthcoming from Spuyten Duyvil Press, and a new poetry collection, *Questions in the Vestibule.* Rachel Hadas's translation of Euripides' *Helen* was published by the Penn Drama Series in 1998; her book of translations, from Ancient and Modern Greek, Latin, and French poetry, *Other Worlds Than This,* was published by Rutgers University Press in 1994. Rachel Hadas's awards include a Guggenheim fellowship, the O.B. Hardison poetry Award from the Folger Shakespeare Library, and an Award in Literature from the American Academy and Institute of Arts and Letters.

HEINRICH HEINE was born in Düsseldorf in either 1797 or 1799. He has been called the last of the Romantics, no doubt because he clearly skirted Romanticism through irony and satire. His university career progressed from Bonn in 1819 to Göttingen in 1820 to the more intellectual climate of the University of Berlin; by 1823 he had fled Berlin as well. When Prussia legislated against Jews taking university posts, Heine converted to Protestantism (1825), saying this was "the ticket of admission into European culture," and changed his name from Harry to Heinrich. In 1831 he took exile in France, anticipating more freedom of speech in view of the new constitutional monarchy there. His next 25 years were spent struggling in Paris despite irregular patronage from an uncle, but developing an international reputation for the lyricism, wordplay, irony, and excoriating wit of his poems. He was well aware of Germany's displeasure with his political statements and satires. In 1841 he married Crescence Eugénie Mirat ("Mathilde"), who spoke no German and could barely read French. Though Heine had a series of mistresses, Mathilde cared for him during his final eight-year paralysis, and he continued to write from bed until his death in 1856. His books would later be burned by the Nazis, creating prophecy out of his statement, "Where they have burned books, they will end in burning human beings." His poems have been set to music by many composers. In keeping with his wishes, his tomb is in Montmartre Cemetery in Paris. In 1997 new analyses of Heine's hair indicated his death had been caused by lead poisoning.

HESIOD is arguably the first writer we know about as a person in Western Literature. Probably writing in the late 8th century BC, he lived in the town of Askra, in Boeotia, Greece (a place he called "miserable in winter, vile in summer, unpleasant all the year round.") He was a farmer himself and won a tripod in a poetry contest. He was embroiled in a lawsuit with his wastrel brother Perses over a property inherited from their father, and complained of corrupt judges; Modern Greeks would recognize this iron-age state of affairs today.

JAY HOPLER's poetry, essays, and translations have appeared most recently, or are forthcoming, in *Ezra: An Online Journal of Translation, Interim, Plume,* and *The Literary Review. Green Squall,* his first book of poetry, won the 2005 Yale Series of Younger Poets Award. His most recent book is *Before the Door of God: An Anthology of Devotional Poetry* (edited with Kimberly Johnson, Yale University Press, 2013). The recipient of numerous honors including fellowships and awards from the Great Lakes Colleges Association, the Lannan Foundation, the Mrs. Giles Whiting Foundation, and the American Academy of Arts & Letters/the American Academy in Rome, he is Associate Professor of English at the University of South Florida.

HORACE (65 BC – 8 BC) was a Roman lyrical poet of satire and historical/pastoral odes. Son of a freedman, eventually he became close friends with Virgil. His famous *Ars poetica* has been an abc of poetry practice and criticism. He was given a farm near Tivoli, and there he wrote his pastoral and other poems. His main works are his *Satires, Odes, Epodes,* and *Epistles.* His *Ars* suggests that a poet should read widely, and be precise and plain in thought and speech. His influence has been enormous on Pope, Ben Jonson, Auden, and Frost. Too often missing is the fact that he is also a passionate, songful poet (as is Catullus, who is also hysterically funny as well as being amorous), and is as moving as William Blake in his poignant portraits. Horace's legacy has largely been limited, because of ignorance of the original text, to the satiric. He remains a world still to be discovered.

VICTOR HUGO (1802 – 1885) is revered as a great Romantic poet and political activist in his native France, but he is better known in the US for his novels, including *Les Misérables* and *The Hunchback of Notre Dame.* The former was brought to stage as musical in London in 1985 and ran on Broadway from 1987 to 2003; the 2012 film adaptation won several Golden Globes and Oscars.

TERESA IVERSON is a poet, translator, and editor. She holds a PhD in German Literature and Literary Translation from Boston University; her dissertation, on the poetry of Gottfried Benn, is titled: *Gottfried Benn's Intimate Discourse: The "Du" in Monologic Art.*

With Rosanna Warren, she taught poetry at MCI-Framingham, Massachusetts' only prison for women, and coedited *In Time*, a collection of student inmates' writing.

Her own poems and translations have been published in many journals, including *PN Review, AGNI, Fulcrum, Arion: A Journal of Humanities and the Classics, Notre Dame Review, New Criterion, Delos, Partisan Review, Poetry Porch, Sonnet Scroll*, and anthologized in *World Literature: An Anthology of Verse from Antiquity to Our Time* (Katherine Walsh and John S. Major, editors). Her translated *Selected Poems of Nelly Sachs* is under review for publication.

NUR JAHAN (1577 – 1645), was the favorite wife of the Mughal emperor Jahangir (1569 – 1627), and the aunt of Mumtaz Mahal, for whom the Taj Mahal was built. She was the most powerful woman in India during much of her husband's reign. The language of the Mughal courts was Persian, and the writing of fluent Persian verse was an expected accomplishment of Mughal courtiers.

ARNOLD JOHNSTON lives in Kalamazoo and South Haven, MI. Cofounder of Western Michigan University's creative writing program and founder of its playwriting program, he taught in the WMU Department of English for many years and served for ten years as its chair. His plays, and others written in collaboration with his wife, Deborah Ann Percy, have won awards, production, and publication across the country. His poetry, fiction, nonfiction, and translations have appeared widely in literary journals and anthologies. His books include *Sonnets: Signs and Portents, What the Earth Taught Us, The Witching Voice: A Novel from the Life of Robert Burns, Of Earth and Darkness: The Novels of William Golding*, and (with Ms. Percy) *Duets: Love Is Strange*. His translations of Jacques Brel's lyrics have appeared in many successful stage revues and on his CD, *Jacques Brel: I'm Here!* He has translated songs by Gabriel Fauré, and his translation of Wilhelm Müller's lyrics for Schubert's *Winterreise* premiered in 2010. He is a member of the Dramatists Guild, the Playwrights' Center, and the American Literary Translators Association.

SOR JUANA INÉS DE LA CRUZ (1648 – 1695), born in San Miguel Nepantla, Mexico, was and remains one of the towering figures of the Spanish Golden Age. A child prodigy with a wide-ranging grasp of literature, languages, science and music, she was famed for her learning and intelligence, as well as her beauty, but choices were limited in New Spain for a woman who wished above all to dedicate her life to scholarship and writing. When she was 21, she entered a convent where she was permitted to maintain her own private study and library for a number of years, and where the leading scholars of her day often came to pay homage and bask in her conversation. She died of the plague in 1695 at the age of 46.

JULIE KANE, the 2011 – 2013 Louisiana Poet Laureate, is a Professor of English at Northwestern State University in Natchitoches, Louisiana. Her most recent poetry collection is *Paper Bullets* (White Violet Press, 2014). Her translations from French and co-translations from Lithuanian have appeared in *Blue Lyra Review, The Drunken Boat, Louisiana English Journal, Nimrod*, and *Druskininkai Poetic*

Fall 2005. She also authored the essay "Francophone Poets of the U.S." in *The Princeton Encyclopedia of Poetry and Poetics*. In July of 2014, the Princeton Singers will premiere Dale Trumbore's musical setting of Victor Hugo's poem "Even as the sailor," with a text translated by Julie.

X.J. Kennedy will have two new books out this year: a comic novel, *A Hoarse Half-human Cheer* (e-book from Curtis Brown Digital, paperback from CreateSpace) and *Fits of Concision: Collected Poems of Six or Fewer Lines* (Grolier Poetry Bookshop). His translations include *The Bestiary* of Guillaume Apollinaire (Johns Hopkins University Press) and the *Lysistrata* of Aristophanes in the Penn Complete Greek Drama series.

Jahan Khanom (1805 – 1873), was the wife (and cousin) of Mohammad Shah Qajar (1808 – 1848), and the mother of Nasraddin Shah Qajar (1831 – 1896), both 19th-century shahs of Iran. After her husband's death in 1848, she briefly acted as regent until her son's coronation. She is credited with having been one of the most politically astute of all the Qajar royal family.

Rima Krasauskytė grew up in Klaipeda, Lithuania. She earned a B.A. in English Philology from Vilnius Pedagogical University (now called "Lithuanian University of Educational Sciences") and an MA in English from Northwestern State University in Natchitoches, Louisiana. Her co-translations from Lithuanian, with Julie Kane, of poems by Tautvyda Marcinkevičiūtė appeared in *The Drunken Boat*. She has taught English at the Lithuanian University of Educational Sciences and at the Military Academy of Vilnius.

Kent Leatham holds an MFA in poetry from Emerson College and a BA in poetry from Pacific Lutheran University. His translations of medieval/Renaissance Scots-language poetry have appeared or are forthcoming from *InTranslation, Rowboat, Anomalous Press*, and *Ezra*. His original poetry has appeared in dozens of journals nationwide, such as *Ploughshares, Fence, Zoland*, and *Poetry Quarterly*. Previously a poetry editor for Black Lawrence Press, Kent currently teaches at California State University Monterey Bay.

Giacomo Leopardi (1798 – 1837), poet, translator, essayist, and philosopher, is considered one of the greatest Italian poets, together with Dante and Petrarch. He grew up in the small town of Recanati, a conservative backwater in Italy's Marche region. His parents were reactionary nobility. His mother was cold, stingy, and committed to not giving Leopardi any money. Besides having squandered much of the family fortune on gambling, his father had spent considerable sums amassing an enormous library of some 20,000 volumes. Tutored at home by priests, the precociously brilliant Leopardi soon exhausted all that these castle pedagogues had to teach, and educated himself in classical and Italian literature and modern languages through his father's library. He wrote extensively and translated Horace and Homer while still in his teens. His classical training permeates his poetry. Through his reading, Leopardi developed a sophisticated philosophy of pessimistic secular realism tinged with a dark romanticism. His advanced ideas soon put him in conflict with his parents, and in 1824 an offer of literary work in Milan allowed him to escape Recanati. So began a series of sojourns in major Italian cities—Bologna, Florence, Pisa—where Leopardi joined intellectual circles, edited, wrote, and expanded his literary reputation, only to be forced, by illness and poverty, to return to Recanati for extended periods. His lyric poems are highly philosophical yet musical meditations on the futility of life, the force of memory, and the hostility of nature. In Leopardi's view, life is essentially tragic and nature is a destructive force. In this, no doubt, he was influenced by his physical infirmities, recurrent bouts of illness, unprepossessing appearance, and utter failure at love. Technically revolutionary, his poetry has been said to include some of the first articulations of modernism, in its sparse use of rhyme, for example, and stark expression of alienation. "To Sylvia" (1828), a mature work, is considered one of his masterpieces. Leopardi finally established himself at Naples, where he died during the cholera epidemic of 1837 at the age of thirty-nine.

KATE LIGHT's poetry collections are *The Laws of Falling Bodies* (Nicholas Roerich Prize, 1997), *Open Slowly* (2003), and *Gravity's Dream* (Donald Justice Award, 2006). A professional violinist, she is also the librettist of *The Life and Loves of Joe Coogan,* an opera based on an episode of *The Dick Van Dyke Show; Once Upon the Wind,* based on a Russian folk tale; and *Einstein's Mozart: Two Geniuses.*

LOPE DE VEGA was born in Madrid in 1562. A poet, dramatist, novelist, and critic, he was also a soldier, and one of the survivors of the tragically misnamed Invincible Armada. He is generally acknowledged as the father of the Spanish drama, and, since his death in 1635, has been widely considered "the Spanish Shakespeare." The poem presented here is drawn from his collection of "Sacred Sonnets."

ANTONIO MALATESTI (1610 – 1672) was a Florentine poet. His collection of riddles, *Una Corona di Enigmi,* was published in 1640. *La Tina,* a sequence of bawdy rustic sonnets, was dedicated to John Milton and presented to him in manuscript; a new edition, edited from this text by Davide Messina, was published in 2014. Malatesti's later verse was collected in the posthumous *Brindisi dei Ciclopi* (1673).

TAUTVYDA MARCINKEVIČIŪTĖ (b. 1954) is a native of Kaunas, Lithuania, with a degree from the Kaunas campus of Vilnius University. She was the 2013 Poezijos Pavasaris [Poetry Spring] Laureate, which is Lithuania's equivalent of the US Poet Laureate position. She has published more than a dozen collections of her poetry and has been honored with the Zigmas Gėlė prize, the Moteris prize, the Kauno Diena award, and several grants from the Lithuanian Ministry of Culture. She was the first English-to-Lithuanian translator of Sylvia Plath, and she has also translated and published poems by Julie Kane, Edna St. Vincent Millay, and Anne Sexton.

MARTIAL, Latin in full MARCUS VALERIUS MARTIALIS (c. 40 – c. 103), was born in the Roman colony on the Iberian peninsula in present-day Spain. He made his way to Rome and chronicled courtly life with epigrams, some of which were bitingly satirical, and others of which were clearly poems-for-hire and occasional verse likely commissioned or written with the anticipation of patronage in return. As the winds of favor shifted, he returned to his native Iberia, where he died.

CHARLES MARTIN—See page viii.

MELEAGER (135 BC – 50 BC) was born in Gadara and lived a long life at the eastern end of the Mediterranean, settling finally in Cos which he described as "the island he loved best." He published a great deal of satirical prose and an anthology of other poets, all lost. What we have are one hundred and thirty four of his own epigrams, celebrating love for pretty women and pretty boys.

MIGUEL DE UNAMUNO (1864 – 1936) was one of the most important intellectuals in Spanish history. Born of Basque parents, Unamuno was a distinguished philosopher, author, and educator. He received his doctorate in philosophy at the University of Madrid and eventually became a professor of Greek language and literature at the University of Salamanca, where he would later serve two terms as rector of the university. The author of numerous books and treatises, Unamuno's creative writings included novels, plays, short stories, and poems.

FOSILDO MIRTUNZIO was the pseudonymous and otherwise unknown author of *Veglie auttunnali* [Autumnal Vigils], published in Venice in 1796. The translations of his two poems in this issue, as well as the two from Malatesti, will appear in the forthcoming anthology *Dancing with the Sphinx: Riddle Poems,* edited by Kate Light and Kathrine Varnes.

R.C. NEIGHBORS is a sixth-generation Oklahoman and current resident of the strange land of Texas. He has studied literature at the University of Arkansas and screenwriting at Hollins University, and he currently serves as a PhD candidate at Texas A&M University with emphases in creative writing and the Native American South. He hopes to leave Texas very, very soon. His work has appeared in *Tampa Review, Barely South Review, Red Earth Review, Parody,* and elsewhere.

LAINE ZISMAN NEWMAN, Dovid's youngest granddaughter, is a PhD student in Drama, Theatre and Performance Studies at the University of Toronto. Her practical and academic work focuses on creating and promoting equitable theatre practices. Her creative and scholarly work has been published in *Canadian Theatre Review; The Rusty Toque; Journal of Dance, Movement and Spiritualties* (forthcoming, 2014); and *Studies in Documentary Film.*

MICHAEL PALMA has published two poetry chapbooks, *The Egg Shape* and *Antibodies;* two full-length collections, *A Fortune in Gold* and *Begin in Gladness;* and an online chapbook, *The Ghost of Congress Street.* His fourteen translations of modern Italian poets include prizewinning volumes of Guido Gozzano and Diego Valeri with Princeton University Press, as well as books by Maurizio Cucchi, Franco Buffoni, Paolo Valesio, Maura Del Serra, and others. His poems, essays, and translations have appeared in many journals and over thirty anthologies. His fully rhymed translation of Dante's *Inferno* was published by Norton in 2002 and reprinted as a Norton Critical Edition in 2007.

GIOVANNI PASCOLI (1855 – 1912), the son of an estate manager, grew up in an idyllic rural setting that was very soon to change. He lost his parents and other members of his family early on in tragic circumstances. Nevertheless, thanks to some financial help, he was able to continue his studies and gain a degree in classics, teaching first in high schools, later in universities. Eventually, in 1906, he was appointed to the chair of Italian Literature at Bologna University recently vacated by his friend and mentor, Giosuè Carducci. Despite his success both as a poet and classicist (he won prizes for his Latin poems), he was troubled by his early traumas and, although trying often to recreate those idyllic youthful conditions in real life, it is in his sometimes nostalgic and often ambiguous poetry that we see a version of traditional rural life that can be perceived in symbolic terms beyond the apparent simplicity. Like Carducci, he was able to adapt classical metres into his poetry, with the addition of rhyme, as here.

He died in Bologna, most probably of cirrhosis of the liver, the result of alcohol abuse.

PAUL THE DEACON (c. 720 – c. 799), during the 780s, was part of the circle of poets and thinkers at the court of Charlemagne, King of the Franks. Apparently descended from a noble Lombard family, Paul later wrote a six-book history of his people and compiled a collection of his homilies at Charlemagne's request.

DEBORAH ANN PERCY, who lives in Kalamazoo and South Haven, MI, earned the MFA in Creative Writing at Western Michigan University. Her chapbook of short fiction, *Cool Front,* appeared in 2010 from March Street Press, and a full-length collection, *Invisible Traffic,* is forthcoming in Fall 2014 from One Wet Shoe Press. Her plays, and those written in collaboration with her husband, Arnold Johnston, have won awards, publication, and production nationwide. Their books include the plays *Rasputin in New York* and *Beyond Sex,* and (with Dona Roşu) translations of Romanian playwright Hristache Popescu's *Night of the Passions, Sons of Cain,* and the *Epilogue.* They have edited a collection entitled *The Art of the One Act* (New Issues Press); and a collection of their own one-acts, *Duets: Love Is Strange* (March Street Press), appeared in 2008. Ms. Percy is a member of the Dramatists Guild, the Playwrights' Center, and the American Literary Translators Association.

FERNANDO PESSOA (1888 – 1935) is generally acknowledged as Portugal's most distinguished and influential poet of the Twentieth Century. Pessoa published his poems under various heteronyms (alter egos with distinctive names and poetic styles). "Autopsicografia," one of Pessoa's most translated poems, was written under his own name, which was itself a kind of heteronym.

FRANCESCO PETRARCH (1304 – 1374) is the great Italian master whose work helped to create the Renaissance sonnet craze in England. He was a priest, a scholar of the Classics, a friend to the great poet Giovanni Boccaccio, and an immensely popular poet in his day. Although a religious professional, he had two children out of wedlock, and is best known for his sonnets professing his intense love for a woman named Laura.

MARIA PICONE is a student at Goddard College's low-residency MFA program and has degrees in philosophy from Rice and Princeton. She taught herself French after she attended a Descartes seminar as an undergraduate, in which she was the only one who couldn't read French. Since then she has read not only philosophy but a wide range of literature in the original. She also has a personal affinity for French because she grew up hearing her grandmother often sing or curse in the language. Maria is also an amateur painter and photographer, whose work can be seen in the forthcoming editions of *The Nassau Review* and *The Pitkin Review,* her school's literary journal.

ARMAND SULLY PRUDHOMME (1839 – 1907) was a student of law and philosophy who worked for years in the office of a Parisian notary after vision problems prevented a career in engineering. His writing efforts, encouraged by Leconte de Lisle, extended the Parnassian style, which objected to both Symbolism and free verse and hoped to restore the classical standards of elegance, calm and impersonality. Despite the small quantity of his verse and essays, Prudhomme was awarded the first Nobel Prize for literature, in 1901.

JOSÉ LUIS PUERTO (b. 1953) was born in the village of La Alberca, in the Sierra de Francia of Salamanca Province. Graduating from the University of Salamanca with a degree in Romance Philology, he served as secretary to Rafael Alberti. In addition to his many volumes of poetry, he has edited several anthologies, translated Portuguese poetry, and produced works of ethnography focusing primarily on folk legends of Northern Spain. He has taught in Sevilla, Segovia and León, where he now resides with his wife María.

Puerto's poetry weds the celebration of sensuality we associate with Neruda with a contemplative insight reminiscent of Rilke: a voice of praise whose plenitude embraces loss, loneliness, mortality, frailty. At once continuum and encounter, his vision is rooted in the landscape of the natural world and the soul's deep cultural memory, where advent has not suffered oblivion: directing our attention to the promise within the dormant seed, he calls us to hearken to the angel of the ordinary. Renunciation and annunciation: the two poles of his world, pulsing with luminous humility.

GIOVANNI RABONI, born in Milan in 1932, worked as an editor and critic. His status as perhaps the greatest Italian poet of his generation is attested to by the inclusion of his complete poems, *L'opera poetica* (2006), in the prestigious Meridiani series of standard Italian authors. He also published several volumes of critical essays, as well as translations of Baudelaire's *Les Fleurs du mal* and Proust's *À la recherche du temps perdu,* among many others. He died in September 2004. *Every Third Thought: Selected Poems 1950 – 2004,* translated by Michael Palma, is forthcoming from Chelsea Editions.

Reshheh, a late 18th- / early 19th-century poet, was the daughter of a famous poet, Hatef of Isfahan. She is considered to be the finest woman poet writing in Persian between the end of the "classical" period of Persian literature in the 15th century, and the mid-19th century.

John Ridland was born in London in 1933. His British parents and he immigrated to California in 1935, where he has lived most of his life. He spent four years at Swarthmore College and two years in the Army in Puerto Rico. In 1956 he returned to Berkeley to study English, met and married Muriel Thomas from New Zealand, a fellow graduate student, and in 1964 completed a PhD from Claremont Graduate University. He taught English at the University of California, Santa Barbara for forty-three years, including nearly three in Melbourne, directing the UC Education Abroad Program in Australia.

Ridland's recent book publications include *A Brahms Card Ballad* (2007), originally published in Hungarian translation in 2004, *Happy in an Ordinary Thing* (2013), and book-length translations of Petöfi's *John the Valiant* (1999) from Hungarian, and the Middle English masterpiece, *Sir Gawain and the Green Knight* (2013). With his essential collaborator, Dr. Peter Czipott, he has been translating modern Hungarian poets, including Sándor Márai's *The Withering World* (Alma Classics, 2013) and Miklos Rádnoti's, as *All That Still Matters at All* (New American Press, 2014). Forthcoming from Askew Publications is an epic, *A. Lincolniad*.

Rainer Maria Rilke (1875 – 1926) born René Karl Wilhelm Johann Josef Maria Rilke, understood the power of words. At a lover's urging, he changed his name to Rainer, which he thought sounded more masculine. He is probably the best-known 20th-century German-language poet, best known for his *Duino Elegies,* his *Sonnets to Orpheus,* and his *New Poems.* In the *Duino Elegies*—his most important work—and his other poems, Rilke combined knowledge of classical literature with a mystical sense of existence and religion. He produced poems that reflected his era while remaining true to what he saw as the loftier ideals that the modern times had rejected. In addition to poetry, he published short stories, plays, and an experimental novel, *The Notebooks of Malte Laurids Brigge.* He died of leukemia in 1926.

Arthur Rimbaud (1854 – 1891) was a French poet who wrote some of the most remarkable poetry and prose of the 19th century. He prefigured surrealism and free verse, and was a major figure in symbolism. Precocious and miserable in provincial France, he ran away to Paris at 16, where he read voraciously and lived in alcoholic squalor, sometimes with Paul Verlaine. Widely regarded as a prodigy, he wrote all of his poetry in the space of less than five years. Before age 21, he burned his last manuscripts and is not known to have written other work. He deserted from the Dutch Army in Java, he was a quarry foreman in Cyprus, then took up the coffee and gun-running trades in Africa. Returning to France for medical treatment on his leg, he died in Marseille at 37, possibly of bone cancer.

Dona Roşu, a Romanian-born poet, essayist, journalist, and translator, lives in Kalamazoo, Michigan. Her work has appeared internationally in such journals as *The American Poetry Review, Poetry,*

Salmagundi, Transilvania, România Literară, San Miguel Writer, and *The Oxford Poetry Review.* Her ten books of poetry, translations, and nonfiction include *Mănăstirea Gura Motrului* (Meridiane, 1969), an art history monograph written in collaboration with her late husband, Lucian Roşu, with photographs by Andrei Pănoiu; *Cineva ne priveşte* (Albatros, 1982), interviews with Romanian biologists, illustrated by Luciana Costea; *Clipe de viată pe alt continent* (Albatros, 1985), profiles of American scientists and cultural figures; and *Letters to My Mother from Her Emigrant Daughter* (Scrisul Romanesc, 2008), her third poetry collection, edited by Kathleen and W.D. Snodgrass and translated by Kathleen Snodgrass and Antonio Costea, Jr. She is a member of the Writers Union of Romania and the Academy of American Poets.

CLAUDIA ROUTON is Associate Professor of Modern & Classical Languages & Literatures at the University of North Dakota. She works with and translates the contemporary literature of Spain. Her work appears in *Absinthe: The New European Writing, Romance Studies, Hunger Mountain, North Dakota Quarterly, Metamorphoses,* and *International Poetry Review.*

NELLY SACHS was born in Berlin, Germany, in 1891, the only child of upper-middle class Jewish parents. As a child, she was partly educated at home because of weak health, and for the same reason her parents discouraged her from a career in dancing, in which she had begun to excel.

In 1906, she first encountered a novel by Swedish author Selma Lagerlöf, with whom she began a correspondence and friendship a year later. Lagerlöf would later help save the lives of Sachs and her mother: the two women escaped on the last plane out of Berlin to Stockholm in May 1940. Sachs lived the rest of her life in Stockholm, most of it in a small apartment shared with her mother, supporting the two of them by translating between Swedish and German.

Sachs's first book was in prose, *Legends and Stories* (1921). She began publishing poems in 1929, although much of her early poetic oeuvre was lost as a result of her emigration. The first of her numerous books of poetry, *In the Dwelling Places of Death,* was published in Berlin in 1947. After her mother's death in 1950, Sachs was institutionalized for mental illness, and though she recovered, continued to suffer periods of paranoia, delusions of Nazi persecution, and hallucinations. Her close friendship with Paul Celan exacerbated their common experience of paranoia.

Her poems, early influenced by German Romanticism, became more mystical, surreal. Sachs also came to speak for the many who had died, stating in her 1966 Nobel Prize acceptance speech: "I represent the tragedy of the Jewish people."

ROBERT SCHECHTER has published poems and translations in *Highlights for Children, The Washington Post, The Evansville Review, String Poet, Poetry East, The Alabama Literary Review, Ironwood, The Raintown Review, Per Contra, Light Quarterly, LightenUp Online, Snakeskin,* and *Bumbershoot,* among other journals.

BILAL SHAW, is a Kashmiri scientist working in quantum information science who completed his PhD at the University of Southern California. In the past he has worked on DNA-based computation and nanotechnology, software architecture, and theoretical self-assembly. He is currently working as a scientist in the Analytics department at ID Analytics in San Diego, where he applies machine-learning techniques to build statistical risk models for fraud and credit space. He is also an accomplished poet.

WENDY SLOAN practiced labor law with the firm of Hall & Sloan before returning to poetry. Her work has been published in journals including *Measure, Mezzo Cammin, The Raintown Review, Blue Unicorn, Big City Lit* and *Umbrella*. Sloan's translations have appeared, or are forthcoming, in *The Chimaera* and *Measure*. She was a finalist in the 2006 Howard Nemerov Sonnet Award Competition.

A.E. STALLINGS is an American poet who has lived in Greece since 1999. Her most recent collection is *Olives*. Her translation of Hesiod's *Works and Days* is forthcoming from Penguin Classics.

GASPARA STAMPA was born in Padua in about 1523 to Bartolomeo and Cecilia Stampa. Her father, a jewel merchant, died in the early 1530s leaving the family impoverished. Cecilia moved to her native city, Venice, where Gaspara and her sister Cassandra became celebrated musicians. The organist Girolamo Parabosco praised Gaspara's "sweet and elegant words" and her "angelic voice that struck the air with its divine accents and made such sweet harmony that it awakened spirit and life in the coldest stones." The scholar and publisher Francesco da Sansovino dedicated several works to Stampa and praised her "most perfect judgement" as a singer of Boccaccio's verse.

Even in her early twenties, Stampa's fame was such that a set of madrigals by Perissone Cambio could be dedicated to her as "a lady of high merit" with the appeal that she should find him "worthy of a place where you place the countless throng of those who adore you, and love your rare talents and beauties."

During the twentieth century a habit grew up of speculating that Stampa may have been a courtesan, although there is no evidence for this and it is far from clear in any case what a courtesan was. The only even half-reliable information we have about her private life and affections appears in the set of over three hundred poems, mostly sonnets and mostly addressed to Count Collaltino di Collalto, which Cassandra published immediately after Gaspara's death in 1554. The sonnets are among the finest female utterances in Western literature.

ZAHARIA STANCU (1902 – 1974) is a celebrated Romanian writer. His novels—*Barefoot, The Gypsy Tribe, Crazy Forest*, and *The Gamble with Death*—have been translated into many languages. His poetry, which he wrote all his literary life, gained its greatest acclaim in his later years, and is distinguished by the simple beauty of its diction and its focus on human mortality and aspirations. Stancu's novels and poems, like those of Thomas Hardy, are complementary parts of an arresting literary vision.

JEFF SYPECK taught medieval literature at the University of Maryland University College for ten years and wrote the 2006 book *Becoming Charlemagne*. Born and raised in New Jersey, he now lives in Washington, DC, where he writes and edits as a contractor for a large government agency.

N.S. Thompson lives outside Oxford, UK. He has contributed essays and poetry to *Able Muse* and many other publications in the UK and USA, including *Agenda, Ambit, Modern Poetry in Translation, New Walk, Stand,* and *The American Scholar.* His books include the verse epistle in rime royal *Letter to Auden* (Smokestack, 2010) and he has coedited a collection of fifteen cantos in ottava rima chronicling the lively adventures of a twenty-first century version of Byron's hero: *A Modern Don Juan: Cantos for these Times by Divers Hands* (Five Leaves, out in September 2014).

Georg Trakl (1887 – 1914) was born in Salzburg, Austria, and seems to have been suicidal in childhood. As an extremely young child, he threw himself first in front of a galloping horse and then in front of a train. When both of those suicide attempts failed, he tried drowning himself in a lake and was rescued only when someone noticed his hat floating away. His adolescence and adulthood were marked by bouts of serious mental illness, drug and alcohol abuse, a supposed incestuous relationship with his sister, and near-constant failure. His first book, *Gedichte* [Poems], was published in 1913. He died a year later in a psychiatric hospital in Krakow where he was sent for observation after the human suffering occasioned by WWI, specifically the battle of Gródek, which brought him to a suicidal mental collapse. Whether his death was the result of suicide or was an accidental overdose of cocaine is still not known. His second book, *Sebastian im Traum* [Sebastian in Dream], was published posthumously.

Paul Valéry (1871 – 1942) was born in Sète on the Mediterranean. As a young man he wrote poems, painted, and was drawn to music and architecture. He studied law, mathematics, and physics at the University of Montpellier before moving to Paris, where his work was noticed by the Symbolist poets of the 1890s. However, searching for a greater understanding of the intellectual and emotional functions of the mind, he withdrew from writing poems for twenty years.

When he returned to poetry, he published *Le Cimètiere Marin,* in 1922, that *annus mirabilis* for modern literature (Joyce's *Ulysses,* Eliot's *The Waste Land,* Frost's *New Hampshire,* and W.C. Williams' *Spring and All*) and art (Picasso's turn from Cubism to Neo-Classicism).

François Villon (1431 – c. 1463) was born François Montcorbier. A promising graduate of the University of Paris, adept in law and the classics, he fled to the countryside in 1455 after killing a priest in a brawl. For the rest of his life he was a violent vagabond, a thief, and arguably the finest lyric poet in French literature. Between imprisonments, in extreme poverty, he produced volumes of poems, including *The Testament*. When his death sentence in Paris was commuted to a ten-year banishment, he left the city and was never heard from again.

John Whitworth, moving effortlessly into old age, has published an indecent number of books of poetry, most with his friend and mentor, the late Harry Chambers; the most recent, *Girlie Gangs,* with the excellent Enitharmon Press. He is published widely in Australia, New Zealand and the United States but lately less so in the UK, where a high-minded atheist, left-leaning muse is gaining ground pretty well everywhere but in *The Spectator,* where his poems still find a home.

Ryan Wilson holds graduate degrees from The Johns Hopkins University and Boston University. Recent work has appeared, or is forthcoming, in a number of magazines, including *32 Poems, First Things, The Hopkins Review, Iron Horse Literary Review, Measure, River Styx,* and *Sewanee Theological Review,* among others. Currently living with his wife in Baltimore, he is a doctoral candidate at The Catholic University of America.

Dovid Zisman (1914 – 1960), a Holocaust survivor, was a poet, playwright and performer in Poland. Known for his poetry in the Lodz ghetto, he was sent to a work camp in the German factory Hasag-Pelcery in Czestochowa in 1943 and later sent to the concentration camp Buchenwald. He wrote and performed his writing during his imprisonment and torture in labor and concentration camps. Following liberation, he married Helen Zisman and continued to write poetry and prose. In 1947, he left Europe to pre-state Israel with his family and years later immigrated to Toronto, Canada, where he owned a fur factory, raised his daughters and continued to act and write. Zisman passed away in Toronto on May 5, 1960, after battling cancer.

Many of Zisman's creative works focus on the social and political experiences and struggles of the Jewish people and his vision of brighter futures. Most recently, his poem *"Rumkowski Litzmannstadt Geto 1943"* was published in an anthology of Holocaust poetry entitled *Słowa pośród nocy* [Words in the Night]. Select poetry is also archived in Yiddish in the Jewish Historical Institute in Warsaw, Poland.

Shifra Zisman, Dovid Zisman's youngest daughter, is a Canadian actress and teacher who performed throughout Canada's east coast in the 1970s as part of the Newfoundland Travelling Theatre Company. As a drama and music consultant, she currently works in Early Childhood Education, and instructs college courses in Toronto, Ontario.

Able Muse Anthology

978-0-9865338-0-8 • $16.95

Edited by Alexander Pepple • *Foreword by* Timothy Steele

PRAISE FOR THE *ABLE MUSE ANTHOLOGY*:

This book fills an important gap in understanding what is really happening in early twenty-first century American poetry. **–Dana Gioia**

You hold in your hands a remarkable anthology of poems, translations, an interview, essays, short stories and visual art. **–David Mason**

This extraordinarily rich collection of fiction, poetry, essays and art by so many gifted enablers of the Muse is both a present satisfaction and a promise of future performance. **–Charles Martin**

Neither unskilled, lethargic, nor distracted from their proper enterprise, the muses in the past decade have been singularly able, as this outstanding anthology from *Able Muse* demonstrates. **–Catharine Savage Brosman**

Here's a generous serving of the cream of *Able Muse*, including not only formal verse but nonmetrical work that also displays careful craft, memorable fiction (seven remarkable stories), striking artwork and photography, and incisive critical prose. **–X. J. Kennedy**

Mark Jarman, Rachel Hadas, Turner Cassity, Stephen Edgar, Timothy Steele, R. S. Gwynn, Rhina P. Espaillat, A. M. Juster, Geoffrey Brock, Annie Finch, X. J. Kennedy, Timothy Murphy, Jennifer Reeser, Beth Houston, Dick Davis, A. E. Stallings, Richard Moore, Chelsea Rathburn, David Stephenson, Julie Kane, Alan Sullivan, Kim Bridgford, Deborah Warren, Diane Thiel, Richard Wakefield, Rose Kelleher, Leslie Monsour, Lyn Lifshin, Amit Majmudar, Len Krisak, Marilyn L. Taylor, Dolores Hayden, Suzanne J. Doyle, Dennis Must, Thaisa Frank, Nina Schuyler, Misha Gordin, Solitaire Miles, and others.

from **Able Muse Press**

Order or, find more information at: **www.ablemusepress.com**
Or, order at: **Amazon.com, BN.com, . . .**
& other popular online & offline bookstores

Able Muse - Winter 2011
Print Edition, No. 12

WITH THE 2011 ABLE MUSE WRITE PRIZE FOR POETRY & FICTION

230 pages
ISBN 978-0-9865338-9-1

Includes the winning story and poems from the contest winners and finalists.

FEATURED ARTIST — Alper Çukur;
(Interviewed by Sharon Passmore)

FEATURED POET — David Mason
(Interviewed by David J. Rothman)

★★★★★

POETRY, FICTION, BOOK REVIEWS, INTERVIEWS & ESSAYS FROM SUZANNE J. DOYLE   CATHARINE SAVAGE BROSMAN   TIMOTHY MURPHY   GABRIEL SPERA   RICHARD WAKEFIELD   SUSAN MCLEAN   LYN LIFSHIN   GEORGE WITTE   AMIT MAJMUDAR   JEAN L. KREILING   RACHEL BENTLEY   DOUGLAS CAMPBELL   ANDREW FRISARDI   DAVID J. ROTHMAN   MICHAEL COHEN   AND OTHERS

ORDER NOW FROM ABLE MUSE PRESS AT: WWW.ABLEMUSEPRESS.COM
OR, ORDER FROM AMAZON.COM, BN.COM, ... & OTHER ONLINE OR OFFLINE BOOKSTORES

www.AbleMusePress.com

Sailing to Babylon
Poems
by James Pollock

*NEW~ *from* **Able Muse Press**

Finalist, 2012, Governor General Literary Awards (Canada)

Shortlisted Book, 2013: The Griffin Poetry Prize

PRAISE FOR *SAILING TO BABYLON* **(with a Foreword by Jeffery Donaldson)**

★★★★★

"Quietly confident, formally adept, assured in their music, these artful lyrics are not only an accomplishment in themselves but promise to register, as the poet says, 'the breaking changes of a life to come'."
— Mark Doty, Judge's Citation, Griffin Poetry Prize shortlist

"... A rich and complex array of subjects and allusions to provide both pleasure and challenge."
—Pleiades: A Journal of New Writing

"In Pollock's unadorned style, forged as it is in traditional forms . . . we get a vision of an old world, freighted with history, and still able to astonish itself with the novelty of its recurrence."
— Michael Lista, The National Post

ISBN 978-0-9865338-7-7 / 80 pages

ORDER NOW FROM **ABLE MUSE PRESS** AT: WWW.ABLEMUSEPRESS.COM
OR, ORDER FROM **AMAZON**.COM, **BN**.COM, . . . & OTHER ONLINE OR OFFLINE BOOKSTORES

www.AbleMusePress.com

INDEX

Symbols

" 'Against the Daily Grind' " 112
"¿Qué tengo yo que mi amistad procuras?" 155
"Τείχη" 8

A

Able Muse Anthology 197
Able Muse Book Award xx, 160, 162, 163, 165, 168, 169, 174, 176
[A Fish Who Wanders through the Garden] 32, 33, 35
Agustini, Delmira 39, 177
Alighieri, Dante 60, 177
"Al Patrulea Cal" 119
"Amen" 81
"Amen" 81
"Amor che ne la mente mi ragiona" 60
"And It Vanishes" 70
Angiolieri, Cecco 36, 37, 38, 177
"Ante un bodegón de Juan van der Hamen" 33
"Ante un cuadro de Jordi Pallarés" 31
"Ante un cuadro de Marc Rothko" 34
"A Silvia" 142
"A Spark of Freedom" 158
"Autopsychography" 1
A Vertical Mile vii, 169
"A Woman's Fear" 138
Ayesheh-ye afghan 52, 53, 178

B

Baer, William 1, 2, 3, 178
Balbo, Ned 4, 5, 7, 178
"Ballade IV from *Les Cent Ballades*" 44
"Ballade LIX from *Les Cent Ballades*" 48
"Ballade LXXXVI from *Les Cent Ballades*" 50
"Ballade VII from *Les Cent Ballades*" 46
Balmain, Melissa vii, xx
Barnstone, Tony 8, 9, 10, 11, 178
Barnstone, Willis x, 12, 14, 16, 18, 19, 21, 22, 24, 179
Baudelaire, Charles 4, 5, 7, 156, 179

Bauer, Mark S. 26, 27, 179
"Before a painting by Jordi Pallarés" 31
"Before a painting by Marc Rothko" 34
"Before a still life by Juan van der Hamen" 33
Berman, Ben vii, xix
Betts, Reginald Dwayne 198
Bradburn-Ruster, Michael 28, 30, 179
Brecht, Bertolt 103, 179

C

Cantor, Michael vii, 168
"Carmen CI" 3
Catullus 3
Catullus, Gaius Valerius 180
Cavafy, C.P. 149, 180
"Cemetery" 130
Chandler, Catherine vii, 39, 171, 180
Char, René 28
"Chestnut Tree" 30
"Chi non sa come dolce il cor si fura" 59
"Chor der Waisen" 84
Christine de Pizan 44, 46, 48, 50, 180
"Circus Performers" 125
"Cleopatra" 24
Coe, Terese 43, 180
"Cold Winter" 16
Compositions of the Dead Playing Flutes vii, 164
Corbett, Maryann vii, 44, 46, 48, 50, 162, 181
Corporeality vii, xii
Corredor-Matheos, José 31, 33, 34, 181
Credo for the Checkout Line in Winter vii, 162
Çukur, Alper 199
Czerwiec, Heidi 31, 33, 34, 181

D

Danish 138
Davis, Dick 52, 181
"Der Schlafwandler" 89
"Die Ratten" 79
Dirge for an Imaginary World vii, 174
Ditlevsen, Tove 138, 182
"Don Juan aux enfers" 5
"Don Juan in Hell" 5
Douglas, Gavin 98, 182
Dubrow, Jehanne 206
Dunbar, William 101, 182

E

Editorial v
Elgar, Adam 55, 56, 57, 58, 59, 182
"*Elle avait pris ce pli*" 92
Eneados 98
"*Engel der Bittenden*" 86
"Enjoy the Day" 18
"*En Kvindes Frygt*" 138
"*Épitaphe*" 70
"Epitaph for the baby Hildegard, daughter of Charlemagne and Queen Hildegard" 150
essay 112
Euripides 74, 182
Evans, Anna M. 206
Evariste, Nicolas 172
"Evening Thunderstorm" 80
"Evil" 95
"Exotic Perfume" 156

F

"*Farfallettina*" 127
"Five Poems" 82
"Five Poems by Women Writing in Persian" 52
"For Monique" 126
Foster, Brett 36, 37, 38, 183
Fowler, William 100, 183
"*Fra l'anschluss e la notte dei cristalli . . .*" 108
French 4, 5, 7, 44, 46, 48, 50, 66, 68, 70, 72, 92, 94, 95, 96, 125, 126, 128, 129, 130, 131, 156
Frisardi, Andrew 60, 183
"from Book 7 of *Eneados*" 98
Furtney, Diane 66, 68, 70, 72, 183

G

Gérard de Nerval 70, 184
German 10, 43, 79, 80, 81, 82, 103
Ghalib, Asadullah Khan 11, 184
"Ghazal 50" 11
Grasshopper: The Poetry of M A Griffiths vii, 170
Greek 8, 74, 145, 149, 153
Griffiths, Margaret Ann vii, 170

H

Hadas, Rachel 74, 184
"Happiness" 43
Heaven from Steam vii, 165
"Heaven's Teeth" 11
"Hedging My Bets" 36
Heine, Heinrich 43, 184
Hesiod 145, 185
"Highhanded Matchmaking" 22
Hopler, Jay 79, 80, 81, 185

Horace 12, 14, 16, 18, 19, 21, 22, 24, 185
"Horace 1.5" 12
"Horace 1.9" 16
"Horace 1.11" 18
"Horace 1.14" 19
"Horace 1.23" 21
"Horace 1.33" 22
"Horace 1.37" 24
"Horace 4.7" 14
House Music vii, 160
Hugo, Victor 92, 185

I

"*I' non vi miro perzar, morditori*" 38
"In Orkney" 100
"Interruption" 149
"Invitation" 21
"*Io assimiglio il mio signor al cielo*" 56
Iphigenia in Aulis 74
"*I' potre' anzi ritornare in ieri*" 36
Italian 9, 36, 37, 38, 55, 56, 57, 58, 59, 60, 105, 107, 108, 109, 110, 142, 151, 152
Iverson, Teresa 82, 185

J

Jahangir 52
Jahan, Nur 52, 186
Johnston, Arnold 117, 119, 121, 186
Juana Inés de la Cruz, Sor 140, 141

K

Kampa, Stephen 173
Kane, Julie 90, 92, 186
Kaufman, Ellen vii, 160
Kennedy, X.J. xx, 94, 95, 96, 187
Khanom, Jahan 52, 187
Krasauskytė, Rima 90, 187

L

"*La casa*" 28
"*La casa di campagna . . .*" 109
"*La Cloche fêlée*" 7
La Sfinge 105
Latin 3, 12, 14, 16, 18, 19, 21, 22, 24, 26, 27, 150
"*La Vie antérieure*" 4
Leatham, Kent 98, 100, 101, 187
"*Le Cimetière marin*" 131
"*Le Lais*" 72
Leopardi, Giacomo 142, 187
"*Le Rendez-vous*" 68
Les Fleurs du mal 157
Le Testament 72
Lieu, Clara 173

Life in the Second Circle vii, 168
Light, Carol vii, 165
Light, Kate 105, 188
Lincoln, Abraham 19
Lindner, April vii, 168
Lines of Flight vii, 171
Lithuanian 90
Lope de Vega 155, 188

M

Malatesti, Antonio 105, 188
"Man at Sunset" 121
Marcinkevičiūtė, Tautvyda 90, 188
Martial 26, 27, 188
"Martial II:53" 26
Martialis, Marcus Valerius 188
"Martial X:33" 27
Martin, Charles viii, ix, 189
Mason, David 199
Meleager 153
"Melon" 129
Miguel de Unamuno 2, 189
Mirtunzio, Fosildo 110, 189
"Mis amores" 39
"My Loves" 39
Myricae 151, 152
"My sad heart snivels on the poop" 96

N

Neighbors, R.C. 103, 189
Nevertheless vii, 171
New and Recent Releases from Able Muse Press vii
Newman, Laine Zisman 158, 189
"Nicht lange täuschte mich das Glück" 43
"November" 152
"Novembre" 152

O

"O Captain, My Captain" 19
"October Evening" 151
"Of the Drowned Girl" 103
Ogbuji, Uche 172
"Om în Amurg" 121
Osen, Frank vii, 176
"O Ship, The Waves Are Sweeping You" 19

P

Palma, Michael 105, 107, 108, 109, 110, 112, 189
"Parcere personis, dicere devitiis" 27
"Parfum Exotique" 156
Pascoli, Giovanni 151, 152, 190
Passmore, Sharon 173, 199
Paul the Deacon 150, 190

Pepple, Alexander v, 197
Percy, Deborah Ann 117, 119, 121, 190
Persian 52
Pessoa, Fernando 1, 190
Petrarch, Francesco 9, 190
Picone, Maria 125, 126, 128, 129, 130, 191
Poèmes variés 72
Pollock, James vii, 200
Ponomarenko, Andrew 198
Poochigian, Aaron vii, 169
"Portugal" 2
Portuguese 1
"Prose Poem" 128
Prudhomme, Armand Sully 68, 191
Puerto, José Luis 28, 30, 191
Pumpkin Chucking vii, 163

Q

"Quand'i' solev'udir ch'un fiorentino" 37
"Quando fra l'altre donne ad ora ad ora" 9
"Quando fu prima il mio signor concetto" 55
"Quatrain" 72

R

Raboni, Giovanni 107, 108, 109, 191
Reshheh 53, 192
"Riddles" 105, 110
Ridland, John 131, 192
Rilke, Rainer Maria 10, 125, 126, 128, 129, 130, 192
Rimbaud, Arthur 66, 94, 95, 96, 192
"Rime 4" 55
"Rime 5" 56
"Rime 8" 57
"Rime 21" 58
"Rime 31" 59
Romanian 117, 119, 121
Roșu, Dona 117, 119, 121, 192
Rothman, David J. 199
Routon, Claudia 31, 33, 34, 193
"Rustic Chapel" 126

S

Sachs, Nelly 82, 193
Sailing to Babylon vii, 200
"Saltimbanques" 125
Scaer, Stephen vii, 163
Schechter, Robert 138, 140, 141, 193
Scots 98, 100, 101
Seamon, Hollis vii, xii
"Se, cosí come sono abietta e vile" 57
"See You, Wouldn't Want to Be You" 38
Señales 30
"Sensation" 94
"Sera d'ottobre" 151

Seth, Vikram x
Shaw, Bilal 11, 194
"She'd Rather Die than Expose Herself to the Outrage of Growing Old" 141
"She Picked Up the Habit" 92
Sílabas del Mundo 29
"S'io, che son dio, ed ho meco tant'armi" 58
Sloan, Wendy 142, 194
Smith, Matthew Buckley vii, 174
Smith, Patricia 198
"Sonet. In Orknay" 100
"Sonnet 13" 9
"Sonnet: In Orkney" 100
"*Sono quello che eravate*..." 107
Sorensen, Barbara Ellen vii, 164
Spanish 2, 28, 30, 39, 140, 141, 155
Stallings, A.E. 145, 149, 194
Stampa, Gaspara 55, 56, 57, 58, 59
Stancu, Zaharia 117, 119, 121, 194
Steele, Timothy 176, 197
Strange Borderlands - Poems vii, xix
"Sunkiausias darbas" 90
Svensson, Peter 206
[Syllables of the World] 29
Sypeck, Jeff 150, 194

T

"Teatime" 126
The Cosmic Purr vii, 169
The Dark Gnu and Other Poems vii, 166
"The Days, The Days" 117
"The Dispossessed" 4
"The Eater of Mandarin Oranges" 127
"The Five Races of Man" 145
"The Fourth Horse" 119
"The Hardest Work" 90
"The House" 28
"The Marriage of Rope and Roof Beam" 37
"The Panther" 10
The Poetics of Translation x
"The Rats" 79
"The Rendezvous" 68
"The Seaside Cemetery at Sète" 131
The Twa Cummeris 101
"The Two Old Nags" 101
This Bed Our Bodies Shaped vii, 168
Thompson, N.S. 151, 152, 195
"To Her Portrait" 140
"Tomorrow" 155
"To Sylvia" 142
[Traces] 30
Trakl, Georg 79, 80, 81, 195
"*Tú,/ En esa vida*" 30
Tufariello, Catherine 172
"Two Epigrams" 153

U

Un pez que va por el jardín 32, 33, 35
Urdu 11

V

Valéry, Paul 131, 195
Veglie autunnali 110
Videlock, Wendy vii, 166, 171
Villon, François 72, 195
Virtue, Big as Sin vii, 176
"Vom ertrunkenen Mädchen" 103
"Vowels" 66
"Voyelles" 66

W

Wakefield, Richard vii, 169
Walking in on People vii, xx
"Walls" 8
"Weathervane" 12
"Wenn der Tag leer wird" 88
"Wenn ich nur wüßte" 82
"What Lasts" 72
Whitman, Walt 19
Whitworth, John 153, 195
Williamson, Greg 173
Wilson, Ryan 155, 156, 196
"Winter Bell" 7
"Winter Breaking Up" 14
Works and Days 145

Y

Yezzi, David xx
Yiddish 158

Z

"Zilele, Zilele" 117
Zisman, Dovid 158, 196
Zisman, Shifra 158, 196

Able Muse - Winter 2013
Print Edition, No. 16

WITH THE 2013 ABLE MUSE WRITE PRIZE FOR POETRY & FICTION

Includes the winning story and poems from the 2013 contest winners and finalists.

FEATURED ARTIST
Peter Svensson

FEATURED POET
Jehanne Dubrow
(Interviewed by Anna M. Evans)

★★★★★

POETRY, FICTION, BOOK REVIEWS, INTERVIEWS & ESSAYS FROM RACHEL HADAS MELISSA BALMAIN RICHARD WAKEFIELD CATHARINE SAVAGE BROSMAN MARLY YOUMANS R.S. GWYNN JOHN SAVOIE D.R. GOODMAN ANNA M. EVANS CHERYL DIANE KIDDER CHARLES WILKINSON A.E. STALLINGS DAVID MASON CHRISSY MASON PETER BYRNE JANE HAMMONS RORY WATERMAN AND OTHERS

192 pages
ISBN 978-1-927409-27-5

ORDER NOW FROM ABLE MUSE PRESS AT: WWW.ABLEMUSEPRESS.COM
OR, ORDER FROM AMAZON.COM, BN.COM, . . . & OTHER ONLINE OR OFFLINE BOOKSTORES

www.AbleMusePress.com

www.ingramcontent.com/pod-product-compliance
Lightning Source LLC
Chambersburg PA
CBHW081847170426
43199CB00018B/2841